THE LEGAL SYSTEM OF COLOMBIA

Library of the Association Henri Capitant

LEGAL SYSTEMS SERIES

★ ★ ★

THE LEGAL SYSTEM OF LOUISIANA

THE LEGAL SYSTEM OF FRANCE

THE LEGAL SYSTEM OF THE NETHERLANDS

THE LEGAL SYSTEM OF ROMANIA

THE LEGAL SYSTEM OF IRAN

THE LEGAL SYSTEM OF QUÉBEC

THE LEGAL SYSTEM OF GERMANY

THE LEGAL SYSTEM OF MADAGASCAR

THE LEGAL SYSTEM OF CAMBODIA

THE LEGAL SYSTEM OF COLOMBIA

THE LEGAL SYSTEM OF UKRAINE

Bibliothèque de l'Association
Henri Capitant

Library of the Association
Henri Capitant

LEGAL SYSTEMS SERIES

THE LEGAL SYSTEM OF COLOMBIA

EDITORS

Alain A. Levasseur
PROFESSOR OF LAW EMERITUS, LSU

Nikolaos A. Davrados
PROFESSOR OF LAW, LSU

Association Henri Capitant

Lextenso

Library of Congress Cataloging-in-Publication Data

Names: Levasseur, Alain A., author. | Davrados, Nikolaos A., author.
Title: The legal system of Colombia / Alain A. Levasseur, Nikolaos A. Davrados.
Description: Durham, North Carolina : Carolina Academic Press, LLC, 2025. | Series: Legal systems series | Includes bibliographical references and index.
Identifiers: LCCN 2025028620 | ISBN 9781531034160 (paperback) | ISBN 9781531034177 (ebook)
Subjects: LCSH: Law—Colombia. | Jurisprudence—Colombia. | Justice, Administration of—Colombia.
Classification: LCC KHH327 .L48 2025 | DDC 349.861—dc23/eng/20250617
LC record available at https://lccn.loc.gov/2025028620

Carolina Academic Press
700 Kent Street
Durham, North Carolina 27701
Telephone (919) 489-7486
Fax (919) 493-5668
www.cap-press.com

Printed in the United States of America

THE SERIES

The Association Henri Capitant has been working to disseminate, modernise and promote civil law for over eight decades.

It has traditionally focused on national and international days and bilateral symposia or seminars, which it organises on a regular basis. As part of the Association's tireless efforts in pursuit of its objectives, its Deputy General Secretary, Cyril Grimaldi, came up with the idea of creating the "Association Henri Capitant Library." The Association's national groups were therefore invited to explain the broad outlines of their law in a series of books, all based on an identical structure, with a limited character count, to give readers the chance to explore and compare the foundations and fundamental features of various systems of law.

As a result, each book in the collection features chapters on the history of the law, its sources, the constitutional framework, legal professionals, criminal law, legal persons, family, property, contracts, liability, quasi-contracts, businesses and labour law.

This provides an invaluable introduction to each system of law, and more besides. Any member of the Association with a username (visit http://www.henricapitant.org to register) can contact the authors of any of the books by e-mail to discuss issues with them (bibliothequecapitant@lextenso.fr).

The new collection is clearly of immense value, giving everyone the opportunity to explore and understand the substance and spirit that make up and inspire the various systems of foreign law featured in the series. Its contribution to comparative law is simply unparalleled; it offers undoubted benefits to all those who understand the value of stepping outside the boundaries of their own law to better appreciate it and draw inspiration from other forms of law to support its development.

Denis Mazeaud
PROFESSEUR, UNIVERSITÉ PANTHÉON-ASSAS

Philippe Dupichot
PROFESSEUR, UNIVERSITÉ PANTHÉON-SORBONNE

Cyril Grimaldi
PROFESSEUR, UNIVERSITÉ PARIS XIII

Alain Levasseur
PROFESSOR EMERITUS, LSU LAW SCHOOL

Randall Trahan
PROFESSOR, LSU LAW SCHOOL

David Gruning
PROFESSOR EMERITUS, LOYOLA LAW SCHOOL

CHAPTER AUTHORS

Mariana Bernal
PROFESSOR
UNIVERSITY OF LOS ANDES
Property

Bernardo Carvajal
PROFESSOR
EXTERNADO UNIVERSITY OF COLOMBIA
Legal Actors

Oswaldo Perez
LAWYER
DEPARTMENT OF COMMERCIAL LAW
EXTERNADO UNIVERSITY OF COLOMBIA
Business Entities, Constitutional Framework, Criminal Law, Legal History

Diego Sanchez
DEPARTMENT OF SOCIAL LAW
EXTERNADO UNIVERSITY OF COLOMBIA
Labor and Employment Law

Katerine Bermúdez
DEPARTMENT OF SOCIAL LAW
EXTERNADO UNIVERSITY OF COLOMBIA
Labor and Employment Law

Jorge Manrique
DEPARTMENT OF SOCIAL LAW
EXTERNADO UNIVERSITY OF COLOMBIA
Labor and Employment Law

Agustin Emane
UNIVERSITÉ DE NANTES
Labor and Employment Law

Silvana Fortich
PROFESSOR
EXTERNADO UNIVERSITY OF COLOMBIA
Contract, Persons, Sources of Law

Margarita Morales
EXTERNADO UNIVERSITY OF COLOMBIA
Contract, The Family

Hector Patiño
PROFESSOR
EXTERNADO UNIVERSITY OF COLOMBIA
Delictual Liability

Javier Rodriguez Olmos
PROFESSOR
EXTERNADO UNIVERSITY OF COLOMBIA
Quasi-Contracts

« THE AUTHORS »

Adriana Rojas
RESEARCHER
EXTERNADO UNIVERSITY OF COLOMBIA
Delictual Liability

Mónica Safar
PROFESSOR
EXTERNADO UNIVERSITY OF COLOMBIA
Contract

Translation
by
Institut Supérieur d'Interprétariat et de Traduction (Paris)

TABLE OF CONTENTS

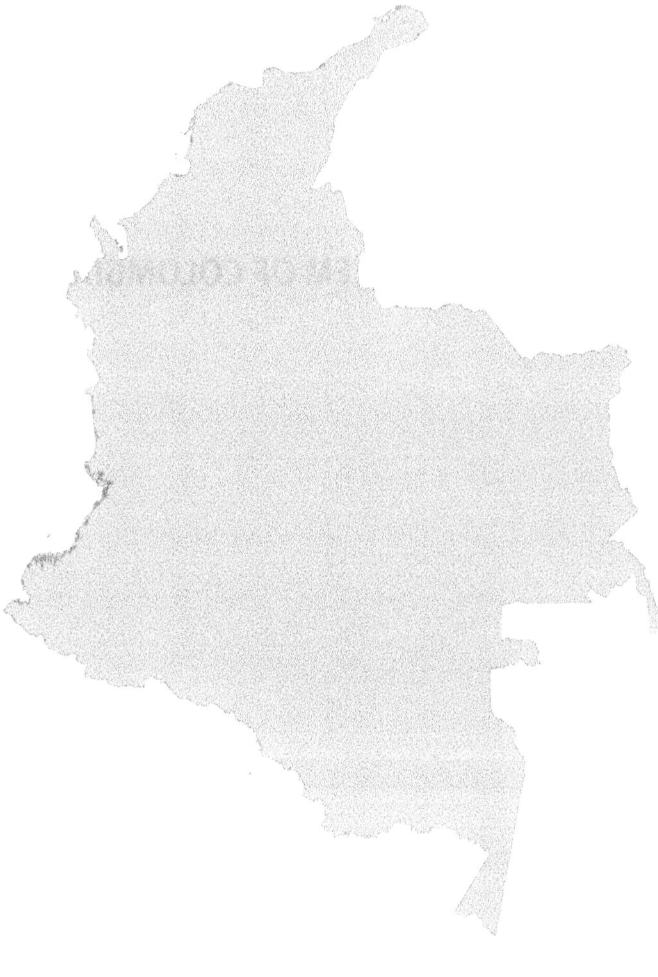

CHAPTER ONE

LEGAL HISTORY

The pre-Hispanic cultures discovered by the Spanish colonisers were not as extensive or dense as those of Mexico or Peru. Thus, New-Grenada (present-day Colombia) was a predominantly Mestizo country, with a relatively small Indian population.

As colonies, theses territories acted as a political, legal (particularly in terms of administrative norms), economic and social satellite of the monarchy. Spanish law included, among others, the Ordinances of Alcalá (1384), the Laws of Toro (1505), the New Compilation of Castile (1567 and 1805), and the Siete Partidas of King Alfonso X (norms of Roman and canonical law). The Laws of the Indies, promulgated by King Carlos II in 1690, constitute a general legal code with a broad and dispersed content (applicable to labour relations, soldiers, viceroys,...) for the benefit of the aboriginal people.

The economy of the *Virreinato* (viceroyalty) was based mainly on gold mining. The peace treaty between Spain and England provided the opportunity to apply a free trade regulation adopted in 1778.

At the end of the colonial period, society was highly hierarchical; however, the process of interbreeding shifted the social order in favour of the revendications of the Creole population.

The separatist aspirations of the *mestizos* were motivated by poor governance by the royal delegates, the independence of the North American people (1775–1783), the collapse of the French royal regime (1789), and the invasion of Spain by Napoleon (1808). A new conception of life in society, oriented towards freedom, and political rights, with political and legal autonomy and the possibility of democratic government, was born.

However, the Act of Independence of the Provinces did not change the existing system but maintained the institutions in force: Socorro (1810), Federation of the United Provinces of New Granada (1811), Tunja (1811), Cundinamarca (1812), Antioquia (1812), Cartagena de Indias (1812), Popayán (1814), Mariquita (1815), Neiva (1815), Pamplona (1815).

Subsequently, three periods can be distinguished in the republican history of Colombia: from the colonial model to an independent state, the path to modernity, and postmodernity.

The break from the colonial model and the structuring of an autonomous administration took place in several stages.

During the first years after independence, Colombia transitioned from colonial administration to a minimal independent government (1819–1850). During this period, Colombia, like its Latin American neighbours, sought both to create and to limit power, following liberal principles in vogue. To this end, it shaped its system by synthesizing the model of the American system and the legacy of a state established by European countries.

Thus, from *Gran Colombia* (union of Nueva Granada and Venezuela, 1819–1830) to *Nueva Granada* (1831–1850), there were three Fundamental Laws (1819, 1821, and 1831) and four Constitutions (1821, 1832, 1843, and 1853).

This period was characterised by political and administrative centralism, as well as liberal-inspired reforms. The principle of the separation of powers was enshrined in the new Republic: the executive, the legislative (two chambers elected by censitary popular vote), and the judiciary. The first constitutions guaranteed freedom of the press, freedom of trade and circulation of goods, and abolished some colonial taxes.

The divergences of opinion in the early years of the Republic gave rise to political cleavages between supporters and opponents of the measures decreed by colonial Spain, as well as between those in favor of or against the ideas of the "Enlightenment." The Liberal Party (merchants and artisans) and the Conservative Party (landowners and families close to the clergy) ensured the transition to the constitution of an independent state. The conditions of this foundation will mark the "historical specificity" of the political parties, which will punctuate the Colombian political system through collaboration, negotiation, or mutual exclusion. The first, following the European tradition, supported the separation of the Church and the State, freedom of worship, and secular education; the second, for its part, defended the Catholic religion as a basic element of the social order, directing civil power.

During the period of the *Confederación Granadina* and the *Estados Unidos de Colombia* (1853–1886), the Constitutions of 1858 and 1863 were adopted, characterized by a federal organization of the state (eight sovereign and independent states with legislative jurisdiction). Slavery and the death penalty were abolished, the first commercial bank was founded, and the national university was reorganized.

The Commercial Code, promulgated in 1853, was based on the Spanish Commercial Code of 1829.

In 1858, the Civil Code of the Republic of Chile (*Andrés Bello*) was adopted by the states of the *Confederación*. This code, inspired by the doctrine and case law that had emerged in France following the promulgation of the French Civil Code, was adopted with adjustments to adapt it to national needs.

In 1885, the Conservative Party, with the support of a faction of the Liberal Party, initiated the *Regeneración* movement. Victorious in the civil war against "radical liberalism" and convened in the National Constituent Council, they approved, a year later, the Constitution of the Republic of Colombia, which remained in force for 105 years.

A single Constitution, revised 71 times, was adopted during this period: the Nation was reconstituted as a unitary and sovereign Republic; the Catholic religion was consecrated as the State religion; the powers of the regions were subordinated to the capital; the Council of State appeared, with advisory, jurisdictional, and administrative oversight functions; and an agency of the administrative function was enthroned.

Law 57 of 1887 unified codification in the new Republic. Henceforth, the following would be in force: the Civil Code of 1873, the Commercial Code of Panama of 1869 and the Maritime Commerce Code of 1884, the Penal Code of the State of Cundinamarca of 1858, the Judicial Codes (procedural) of 1872 and 1874, as well as the current Fiscal and Military Codes.

The French influence in administrative law is significant: in 1910, a specialized judge was established, and from Law 130 of 1913, the Council of State obtained jurisdictional control over all administrative activities. Independent administrative authorities emerged with Law 58 of 1931, creating the *Superintendencia de Sociedades Anónimas*, to supervise corporations/limited companies and foreign companies established in Colombia.

Furthermore, Decree 2158 of 1948 and Law 6 of 1945 were the first attempts to codify labor law, regulating individual work/employment contracts, freedom of association, collective bargaining, and social benefits. The Labor Code was adopted in 1950, viewing work as a social obligation and guaranteeing social rights and protections (rights to strike, assembly, association...). Then, Decree 2351 of 1965 introduced, notably, the importance of indefinite-term contracts and effective trade union protection.

Judicial activity was reorganized in 1964, delineating competencies between the Council of State and the Supreme Court of Justice.

The 1971 Commercial Code was inspired by the Italian Code of 1942, the Mexican Code of 1934, the Japanese Code of 1951, and the French Companies Law of 1966.

Politically, the Conservative Party monopolised the political scene during the first Conservative Republic, throughout a long period of hegemony (1886–1930). The Industrial Revolution era corresponds to the second Liberal Republic (1930–1946), during which the Liberal Party formed homogeneous governments. From

1949, during the second Conservative Republic (1946–1953), repression of strong dissent in the countryside ignited several regions of the country and compelled the Liberal Party to abstain from participating in elections, "lacking guarantees."

After these alternations and in order to put an end to the era of *violencia*, the parties established a *constitutional dictatorship*, which was overturned by a *coup of opinion* in 1957. The traditional parties reconciled once again, with the agreement of the "National Front," a kind of republican pact ratified by the Colombian people through a referendum. This pact stipulated mandatory alternating of the presidency between the Liberal and Conservative parties every four years for sixteen years (1958–1974), as well as equal representation in Congress, departmental assemblies, municipal councils, the Supreme Court of Justice, ministries (except for the Ministry of Defense, held by a military officer), and most administrative positions.

Such institutionalization of bipartisanship led other parties to participate in elections under one of the "two flags," but the political system continued to be perceived as "blocked." Several attempts by Congress to reform the charter failed, prompting the search for other mechanisms through routes not provided for in the Constitution.

The 1991 Constitution was adopted through a legally irregular but politically legitimized procedure: the recourse to the primary constituent. Again, in Colombian political history, a coalition—composed by the Liberal Party, certain sectors of the Conservative Party, and the M-19 movement—formed to establish another legitimacy of power on new bases and to make possible constitutional reforms as instruments of national reconciliation.

Thus, the political system was reconfigured, after several revisions of the electoral regime, to make way for a coalition system, in which seven parties occupy center stage.

In the new Constitution, 380 permanent articles and 60 transitional articles ratify the concept of a unitary, decentralized state with a certain degree of local autonomy. This charter adopts an extensive catalog of fundamental rights, providing the means to make them enforceable. Representative democracy is complemented by a participatory democracy (with mechanisms of semi-direct democracy).

The concept of constitutional prevalence has been materialized by the creation of a Constitutional Court. In administrative matters, the Constitution introduces a new nomenclature of "public servants" exercising an "administrative function," along with the "objective" responsibility of the state. The contentious administrative jurisdiction is strengthened to resolve conflicts between citizens and the administration, through the Council of State and, at local levels, through tribunals and administrative judges.

The new Constitution also allows for the transformation of the penal system from an inquisitorial to an accusatory model, with the creation of the *Fiscalía general de la Nación*, a body responsible for investigation and inquiries in criminal matters, as well as the establishment of a Superior Council of the Judiciary, managing administrative, disciplinary, and professional aspects of judges and the institution of the *Defensor del pueblo* to defend fundamental rights.

Regarding social law, the new Constitution introduced social security and the right to work as fundamental rights; which led to the adoption of a new concept of social protection in Law 789 of 2002 and the adoption of flexible working hours.

Subsequently, Colombian legislation has adapted to the demands of the twenty-first century: this includes the modernization of administrative careers (Law 443 of 1998), gender equality (Law 823 of 2003), corporate law (Law 1258 of 2008 introducing simplified joint-stock companies or SAS), the voting rights of foreigners (Law 1070 of 2006), the protection of personal data (Law 1581 of 2012), the prohibition of the commercialization of human organs (Law 919 of 2004), animal protection (Law 1776 of 2016 recognizing their rights), the fight against terrorism (Law 1121 of 2006), and means to end the armed conflict (Law 434 of 1998, creating the National Council of Peace; Law 497 of 1999, establishing peace judges; Law 1745 of 2014, creating mechanisms to end the armed conflict; Law 1732 of 2014, establishing the Chair of Peace in public schools). More recently, laws have been approved: Law 1778 of 2016 on measures to combat international corruption; Law 1931 of 2018 with directives to fight climate change; Law 2064 of 2020 on measures to combat the Covid-19 pandemic; Law 2028 of 2021 governing remote work and Law 2085 of 2021 revising the laws in force to date.

CHAPTER TWO

SOURCES OF LAW

The sources of law can be defined as the causes giving rise to the law; everything that originates law, what produces it. For Kelsen, the sources are not different from the law itself, they are the same legal norms. Faced with the multiplicity of sources of law, authors have created various classifications.

Most authors agree to classify them into material or real, formal, and historical sources. Material or real sources are the factors or elements that determine the content of norms, for example, social, economic necessities, and problems. Formal sources, on the other hand, can be defined as the processes of manifestation of legal norms, everything that has the potential to create law; or as the means of expression of the law. Finally, historical sources are the set of documents or laws that have influenced the drafting of another law.

Other authors have also made a distinction between written and unwritten sources.

Among the written sources, the law is the formal source par excellence. Article 4 of the Colombian Civil Code states that the law is a declaration of sovereign will, respecting the forms required by the Constitution. In this sense, the law can order, prohibit, permit, or punish.

In a ruling on 4 September 1970, the High Civil Court of the Colombian Supreme Court of Justice established that the law is any act of the State containing a rule of objective positive law. The law has a general, abstract, and impersonal character.

The law is compulsory in that it is imposed on everyone, and that non-compliance entails sanctions. It must come from the authority that has the legitimate power to produce them. In Colombia, the body responsible for producing the law is the Congress of the Republic, formed by two chambers: the Senate and the House of Representatives. Its website offers a service for consulting current bill projects and laws in force (http://www.secretariasenado.gov.co/).

Furthermore, the law is general in its application as it is established for an indeterminate number of recipients, which implies that it has *erga omnes* effects. Finally, the law is a permanent rule, meaning that it is compulsory from its creation until its extinction.

Regarding its promulgation, the law generally comes into force for the future, indefinitely in time. Once promulgated, the laws have a general and immediate effect in time, meaning that the retroactive application of the law is prohibited in Colombian law. Indeed, articles 17 and following of Law 153 of 1887 establish that laws cannot affect rights previously obtained under the influence of a former law and that mere expectations do not constitute a right under the new law. Ruling C-147 of 19 March 1997, by the Colombian Constitutional Court, lists the definitions and differences between the notions of *acquired rights* and *mere expectations*. Similarly, in a ruling by the Colombian Supreme Court of Justice (high court of ordinary justice) on 14 June 1969, Justice Eustorgio Sarria established norms of application concerning "acquired rights" and civil status.

According to the terms of article 8 of the Civil Code, even if by the effects of time a law is no longer used or becomes obsolete, it is still in force. The application of the law can indeed be suspended only by the express manifestation of the will of the legislator, by the declaration of a state of exception, or by the provisional suspension established by administrative courts.

The law loses its force following the revocation of its validity, through the process of derogation. It should be noted that a law can only be derogated by another law of the same or higher nature and hierarchy, and that derogation of the law can be total—abrogation—or partial, express or tacit.

Furthermore, regarding the rules for the application of the law in space, article 18 of the Civil Code affirms the principle of territoriality of Colombian law, stipulating that the law is obligatory for nationals and foreigners residing in Colombia. In turn, article 19 of the Civil Code establishes the principle of extraterritoriality of the law in matters of civil status, capacity, and obligations related to family law. Additionally, article 20 of the same code states that in matters of real estate located in Colombia, Colombian law applies.

Concerning the hierarchy of sources of law and the position of the law within this hierarchy, according to Article 4 of the 1991 Colombian Political Constitution, the Constitution is the norm of norms; therefore, in case of incompatibility between the Constitution and the law, or any other legal norm, the constitutional provisions apply. In this sense, the Constitution is the foundational norm in the Colombian system of sources of law, offering unity, cohesion, and validity to the entire legal order.

According to Hans Kelsen's studies, there is a tiered construction of the legal order. Thus, the legal order is represented as an inverted pyramid, with the base being the Constitution, the foundational norm, from which all other lower hierarchy norms descend. Consequently, vertical and horizontal compatibility between the different norms of the system is necessary: vertical compatibility implies that lower norms must respect the limits established by higher norms, while horizontal compatibility involves harmony between norms of equal value.

Colombian law has embraced the Kelsenian hierarchy, establishing that the base norm, the foundational norm, is the Political Constitution, from which emanate the other norms of the legal system.

In other words, the Political Constitution is the norm of norms, the law of laws, and, in this sense, it can be understood within the notion of law in a broad sense. Therefore, article 10 of the Colombian Civil Code establishes that, in case of incompatibility between a constitutional norm and a legal norm, the former must apply. This article, along with articles 1 and following of Law 153 of 1887, determines the criteria for resolving vertical and horizontal incompatibilities between the different norms of the legal system.

Regarding the relationship between the law and other sources of law, Article 230 of the Political Constitution states that judges, in the exercise of their functions, are bound only to the law. Equity, jurisprudence, general principles of law, and doctrine are only auxiliary sources. In this sense, in terms of sources of law, Colombian law follows the system of countries of the Romano-Germanic tradition, also known as civil law, according to which the law is the principal source while jurisprudence, doctrine, and general principles of law are secondary sources.

Another written source of Colombian law is jurisprudence. It can be defined as the set of doctrines and principles contained in the decisions of the state's high courts.

Jurisprudence is a formal source of law in that it is enunciated by official organs of the state. For rulings to be considered jurisprudence, they must be produced by high courts, namely the Supreme Court of Justice, the Constitutional Court, or the Council of State. To consult jurisprudence, one must go to the official website and search according to the branch of law (http://jurisprudencia.ramajudicial.gov.co/WebRelatoria/consulta/index.xhtml).

According to the terms of Article 230 of the Political Constitution, jurisprudence is, in principle, only an auxiliary source of law, as it applies only in cases of legislative lacunae or in the presence of an obscure law; thus, it produces effects inter partes. Article 17 of the Civil Code states that judicial decisions are endowed with obligatory force only in the specific cases that provoked them. This article establishes a general prohibition of regulatory rulings.

However, rulings emanating from a constitutional review, enunciated by the Constitutional Court, generate jurisprudence of an obligatory nature and produce *erga omnes* effects.

Thus, according to Article 243 of the Colombian Political Constitution, rulings of the Constitutional Court enjoy the effects of constitutional *res judicata*. For this reason, the rulings of the Constitutional Court, unlike those of other courts, produce *erga omnes* effects.

In this sense, according to ruling C-820 of 4 October 2006, by the Constitutional Court, the interpretation of the law—article 25 of the Civil Code—, made by this court within the framework of constitutional control, is obligatory. Regarding "tutelage rulings"—for the protection of fundamental rights—, the Constitutional Court stipulates that they produce inter partes effects; however, their reasoning has *erga omnes* effects in that the arguments used by the Court are considered constitutional doctrine.

Consequently, the rule of jurisprudential precedent applies in constitutional matters. In this sense, the rulings of the Constitutional Court are obligatory and produce *erga omnes* effects. The fundamental reasons laid out by the constitutional court for admitting the rule of jurisprudential precedent are the principle of material equality and the principle of legal security, assured by the notions of material *res judicata* and legitimate trust in the administration of justice.

Regarding the incorporation of the rule of jurisprudential precedent in Colombian law, recent laws, in administrative matters, have introduced norms recognizing obligatory force to jurisprudence. On the one hand, Law 1395 of 2010 stipulates that public officials must respect the jurisprudential precedents in ordinary and administrative matters, produced on the occasion of five or more analogous litigations. On the other hand, Law 1437 of 2011—Administrative Code—consecrates the figure of the extension of the jurisprudence of the Council of State, thus developing the obligation for administrative authorities to respect the unification rulings of this court.

Finally, the new Administrative Code enshrines the extraordinary recourse of unification of jurisprudence, seeking to ensure the unity of the interpretation of the law, its uniform application, and to guarantee the rights of the parties and third parties affected.

Doctrine is another written source of Colombian law. It consists of the set of theories and scientific studies contained in books, treatises, and journals, which contribute to the interpretation of positive law and guide legislative reforms.

Doctrine represents the scientific studies published by jurists with the purpose of interpreting the norms and establishing their rules of application. According to Article 230 of the Political Constitution, doctrine is one of the auxiliary criteria of judicial activity, in case of a gap or obscurity in the law.

Let us now set aside written sources and move on to the study of unwritten sources of Colombian law.

Custom is a repeated behavior. If it meets certain conditions, custom can have the force of an autonomous source of law. Indeed, article 13 of Law 153 of 1887 affirms that general custom conforming to morality constitutes law in the absence of positive legislation.

There are several types of customs. Firstly, *secundum legem* custom is that which is formed in harmony with the provisions of the law. Secondly, *praeter legem* custom is that which fills the gaps in the law; it is an unwritten norm, which does not contradict the law but completes it; it is thus understood among the auxiliary sources of the law. And, thirdly, *contra legem* custom is that which is contrary to legal provisions. According to article 8 of the Civil Code, *contra legem* custom does not have force against the law.

Article 3 of the Commercial Code states that commercial custom has the same authority and force as the law, provided it is not contrary to legal provisions and if the constitutive facts of the custom are public, uniform, and reiterated.

While Article 230 of the Political Constitution does not mention custom as an auxiliary source of law, jurisprudence, for its part, has reiterated its character as a source of law, with rulings C-486 of October 28, 1993, and C-224 of May 5, 1994, by the Colombian Constitutional Court.

Finally, general principles of law are enshrined by Article 230 of the Political Constitution as an auxiliary source of law. These principles fulfill various functions: creation, interpretation, and integration of the norm.

Among these general principles of law, it is possible to mention good faith, abuse of right, unjust enrichment, and equity.

CHAPTER THREE

THE CONSTITUTIONAL FRAMEWORK

Colombia, one of the oldest democracies on the continent, has experienced a relatively stable system despite numerous episodes of violence since its independence in 1819.

In 1991, a Constituent Assembly replaced the 1886 Constitution, which had, beyond its revisions (71 in total), nearly 105 years of existence. This new Constitution retained the essence of the democratic system, introducing new institutions: the enshrinement of a new Charter of Fundamental Rights, the introduction of a political reform ensuring broader pluralism and the adoption of mechanisms for citizen participation, the modification of public powers, and the introduction of greater local autonomy, among others.

The text, modified by 56 constitutional revisions to date, including six related to the peace agreements with the FARC (2016), retained the presidential system, based on a strong separation of powers and largely inspired by the American model, while introducing elements of a parliamentary system.

1. CONSTITUTION

The preamble of the Constitution aims at the following objectives: strengthening the unity of the Nation, ensuring the life, social cohesion, work, justice, equality, education, freedom, and peace of the citizens, all within a legal, democratic, and participatory order, guaranteed by a just political, economic, and social order.

1.1 MAIN CHARACTERISTICS OF THE CONSTITUTION

The Constitution grants rights to citizens against public authorities (dogmatic part), provides for their organization (organic part), but also ensures that the guarantee of their activities is subject to the law (Rule of Law).

Thus, a wide range, though not exhaustive, of rights and freedoms has been enshrined:

- *Classical rights*: rights to life, reputation, equality, peace, personality, privacy; freedoms of conscience, worship (which changed the confessional nature of the former Constitution towards a secular state), expression, information, education, association, movement, and work;
- *Social rights*: family rights, divorce rights, gender equality, protection of children and adolescents, access to healthcare services and decent housing;
- *Economic rights*: guarantee of private property, as well as economic activity and private initiative;
- *Cultural rights*: freedoms of teaching, access to culture, artistic expression, free official education, academic autonomy; rights to the creation and protection of intellectual property;
- *Collective rights*: participation of consumer associations, citizen participation in administrative decisions, planning of natural resources, protection of public spaces;
- *Minority rights*: special constituency of two seats in the Senate for indigenous communities; nationality of members of communities in border territories; recognition of ethnic and cultural diversity; regulation of collective ownership of Afro-descendant communities.

Simultaneously, the Constitution ensures the means to enforce these rights through the tutela procedure, the cumplimiento procedure, and the popular action procedure:

- Through the *tutela* action, any person has the possibility to approach the judge, through a summary procedure, to claim the protection of their fundamental rights violated or threatened by a public authority or by the action or omission of another person responsible for the provision of a public service, when there is no other means of defense (subsidiary action);
- Through the *cumplimiento* action, citizens have the opportunity to approach the administrative judge to obtain the fulfillment of a duty omitted by public authorities or by persons exercising public functions;
- Through the *popular* action, citizens can assert their collective rights and interests (indivisible goods, not susceptible to individual appropriation, shared by a plurality of individuals) against the action or omission of public authorities. The constitutional norm defines collective rights as those attached to public heritage and administrative morality, in addition to the rights of consumers of public services.

Correlatively with rights, the Constitution provides for a catalogue of duties: to respect the rights of others and not to abuse one's own rights, to act with the goal of social solidarity, to support public authorities in defending national integrity, to defend human rights as the foundation of peace, to participate in social life, to collaborate with the administration of justice, to protect the financial, cultural, and natural resources of the country, to contribute to the financing and expenses of the State in justice and equity, to fulfill military obligations, among others.

1.2 STRUCTURE OF THE STATE

Article 1 of the 1991 Constitution defines the State as a "social rule of law [according to the Constitutional Court, in a decision of 11 May 1993, formal subjection to the law is complemented by subjection to substantive social content], organized in the form of a unitary, decentralized, democratic, participatory, and pluralistic Republic, based on respect for human dignity, work, and solidarity, with the prevalence of the general interest."

According to Capitant (a French jurist and politician of the 20th century), the State is a group of individuals established in the same territory and subject to the authority of a government.

It is possible to attribute nationality and citizenship to inhabitants. The former is the legal and political bond that grants an individual the status of a citizen of a State; Colombia combines the criteria of *jus sanguinis*, *jus soli*, and *jus domicilii* to grant nationality by birth or adoption. The latter is obtained at 18 years old, allows the exercise of political rights, and entails rights and obligations.

The territory, on the other hand, is represented by the terrestrial space, defined by the borders established by international treaties or defined by arbitral decisions, the subsoil, the airspace, the territorial sea, the submarine platform, and the geostationary orbit.

The public authorities are formed by all the institutions empowered to exercise authority.

2. CONSTITUTIONAL POWERS

All Colombian Constitutions have retained the traditional powers: legislative, executive, and judicial. The 1991 text also maintained these traditional organs while adding certain independent bodies.

2.1. LEGISLATIVE POWER

The legislative power is exercised by a bicameral Congress, elected for four years. The Senate, composed of 108 members, includes: 100 senators from a single national constituency, two representatives of indigenous communities, five senators designated by the *Fuerza Alternativa Revolucionaria del Común* (FARC) party under the 2016 peace agreements, and one seat allocated to the candidate for the presidency who was defeated in the last elections.

Out of 172 representatives in the lower Chamber, 161 are elected by departmental territorial constituencies, two represent Afro-descendant communities, and one represents indigenous communities. Additionally, there is an international constituency representing Colombians abroad, a special constituency for the territories of San Andrés, five senators designated by the *Fuerza Alternativa Revolucionaria del Común* party under the 2016 peace agreements, and one seat allocated to the candidate for the vice presidency who was defeated in the last elections.

The Chambers meet during two annual sessions from July 20 to December 16 and from March 16 to June 20. They can also convene in an extraordinary session at the request of the President of the Republic. The Congress meets as a single body for the opening and closing of sessions, to grant powers to the President of the Republic, receive foreign heads of state, elect the Vice President and the Contralor (General Comptroller), as well as decide on motions of censure against ministers.

Seven constitutional commissions are authorized to examine in first reading bills originating from the executive or parliamentarians (there is hardly any conceptual difference between a proposal and a bill). To facilitate and specialize the functions of Congress, there are also legal commissions (human rights, ethics, and parliamentary status) and special commissions (monitoring control bodies, electoral organization, and decentralization).

In addition to the representation function, the legislative power exercises the function of making law, through constitutional laws (the Constitution can also be revised by a constituent assembly or by referendum) or through laws (organic, statutory, framework, ordinary).

The legislative power also exercises a control function. This is political when it summons ministers and other senior state officials for questioning. If this leads to a motion of censure, it can engage the individual responsibility of ministers or conclude with an *observation motion*. This control can also be judicial when it aims to judge the President of the Republic through impeachment;

for this purpose, the House of Representatives accuses the head of state before the Senate for "acts or omissions in the exercise of his duties."

Finally, the legislative power also exercises an electoral function concerning the General Comptroller, the Attorney General, the justices of the Constitutional Court, the *Defensor del Pueblo* (Citizen's Defender), and, in case of permanent vacancy, the Vice President.

2.2. EXECUTIVE POWER

The President of the Republic and the Vice President are elected by direct universal suffrage in two rounds for a four-year term. The President of the Republic combines the functions of head of state, head of government, and supreme administrative authority.

The dominance of the presidential institution extends beyond the distribution of powers, as it leaves its mark on the entire political system. Thus, the President is not politically accountable to Congress, and cannot dissolve it.

The Vice President replaces the President during their temporary or permanent absences.

The President, the Council of Ministers, and the heads of administrative departments form the government. Ministers carry out both political functions (communication with Congress, presentation of bills, participation in debates, and answering questions before the Chambers) and administrative functions (exercise of functions delegated by the President, coordination of institutions under their jurisdiction, etc.).

Ministers may face individual motions of censure, resulting in the suspension of the official's duties.

In the centralized structure of the national administration, in addition to ministry services, there are administrative departments responsible for technical functions and capable of being delegated executive functions.

Among the decentralized entities, mention can be made of: (1) special administrative units (responsible for executing programs of ministries and administrative departments), (2) public establishments (having legal personality and administrative autonomy, responsible for administrative functions and the provision of public services), (3) state social enterprises (created by the Nation or territorial entities, directly providing public health services), (4) state industrial and commercial enterprises (engaged in industrial or commercial activities and economic management according to private law standards), (5) home public service enterprises (aiming to provide these services), and (6) mixed economy companies (constituted by private contributions and engaged in industrial or commercial activities subject to private law standards).

Superintendencias (superintendencies)—independent administrative authorities—are bodies created by law, possessing administrative and financial autonomy, legal personality or not, inspection functions, surveillance, and, possibly, jurisdictional functions. Among them are the *superintendencia* of banks, the superintendence of companies, and the superintendence of public services.

There are also other autonomous and independent public powers, established by the Constitution to fulfill the functions of the State: the Public Ministry (Attorney General and Citizen's Defender), the General Comptroller (functioning as the Court of Auditors), the Attorney General (responsible for criminal case investigations), and the Electoral Organization.

2.3. JUDICIAL POWER

The ordinary (common law) jurisdiction is exercised by the Supreme Court of Justice, regional superior courts, and judges (civil, labor, criminal, family, and multiple competences). Administrative jurisdiction is composed of the Council of State, regional administrative courts, and administrative judges. Finally, constitutional jurisdiction is grouped in the Constitutional Court.

The Supreme Court of Justice is composed of 23 magistrates, elected by co-option of candidates presented by the Superior Council of the Judiciary, for a period of eight years. The highest jurisdiction includes five chambers: a plenary chamber, a government chamber, a civil and agricultural cassation chamber, a social cassation chamber, and a criminal cassation chamber.

The Supreme Court has the mission of acting as a Court of Cassation, in order to ensure the correct application of the law by the courts (Courts of Appeal), to guarantee a uniform interpretation of the law, to judge the President, high-ranking state officials, and members of Congress, as well as to resolve disputes involving diplomatic agents.

The Council of State is both the highest administrative court and an advisory body to the government. It is composed of 31 judges appointed by co-optation from the candidacies submitted by the Superior Council of the Judiciary and is divided into five sections and a chamber of Consultation and Public Service.

According to the Constitution's Article 237, the Council of State is the highest administrative jurisdiction, in accordance with the rules provided by law, and is competent to hear actions for annulment due to the unconstitutionality of decrees issued by the government (this competence does not belong to the Constitutional Court). It also acts as the supreme advisory body of the government in administrative matters, prepares and submits proposals for amendments to the Constitution, draft laws, and hears cases of the removal of mandates of members of Congress.

The Constitutional Court is composed of nine judges, elected by the Senate from the nominations submitted by the President of the Republic, the Supreme Court, and the Council of State, for a period of eight years.

The Constitutional Court is competent (1) to decide on appeals for annulment due to unconstitutionality filed by citizens against laws amending the Constitution (procedural errors), (2) to decide on the constitutionality of a referendum or the convening of a constituent assembly (formal errors), (3) to decide on appeals for annulment due to unconstitutionality filed by citizens against laws (substantive and procedural defects), (4) to decide on appeals for annulment due to unconstitutionality against decrees with the force of law issued by the government (material and procedural errors), (5) to rule on the constitutionality of contested bills by the government, (6) to decide on the constitutionality of international treaties and the laws approving them, and finally (7) to review judicial decisions related to requests for the protection of fundamental rights (*tutela* action).

Thus, any citizen can make use of constitutional litigation, through an action or exception, in a procedure, before any judge.

CHAPTER FOUR

LEGAL ACTORS

1. MAGISTRATS-JUDGES

In Colombian law, judges are state officials tasked with resolving disputes submitted by parties to a given jurisdiction (administrative contentious, civil ordinary, etc.) in complete independence and impartiality. They ensure the essential public service of administering justice, even though the 1991 Constitution does not grant them a monopoly on adjudication. Indeed, alongside judges who are officials of the Colombian judicial organization, there are administrative authorities and individuals authorized by law to render decisions with the force of judgments in certain areas (such as some independent administrative authorities, military tribunals, and justices of the peace), as well as private arbitrators authorized by law and the will of the parties to resolve certain disputes.

Here, we focus on a strict sense definition of judges, namely that of the judge-official within the Colombian judicial organization, in accordance with the Law on the Administration of Justice (Law 270 of 1996). It should be noted first that due to the administrative decentralization characterizing the judicial organization, there are, on one hand, judges whose jurisdiction is exclusively exercised within geographically delimited territories predefined by law. These are single judges, ruling within a jurisdictional circuit (trial judges), as well as panels of judges (tribunals composed of magistrates), ruling within a jurisdictional district, which itself encompasses several jurisdictional circuits.

Trial judges (municipal judges and circuit judges) render decisions either in single instance or as the first instance of jurisdiction, while district courts constitute the second instance jurisdiction, although the law may assign them first instance competences, as is the case for administrative tribunals.

On the other hand, there are the highest magistrates, who are part of the high courts of justice (Constitutional Court, Council of State, Supreme Court of Justice) and whose jurisdiction extends over the entire Colombian territory.

Generally, all the competences of judges and magistrates are conferred by the Constitution (concerning only the high courts) and more specifically by laws, including procedural codes in different areas of law (for example, the General Code of Procedure, Criminal Procedure Code, Administrative Procedure Code). The rule, in terms of attributing competences to judicial authorities, is that of regulated competence, which generally prohibits purely discretionary competences, as judges and magistrates are competent only in matters designated by procedural law.

In the absence of competence explicitly or implicitly attributed by the Constitution or the law to a given judge or tribunal, the Colombian Law on the Administration of Justice of 1996, as well as the new General Code of Procedure, provides that competence defaults to the civil ordinary judge (civil judicial jurisdiction). This ensures ultimately that every dispute always has its natural judge.

Regarding the recruitment method, it should be noted that trial judges (municipal and circuit judges), as well as magistrates of district courts, are career civil servants recruited through competitive examinations. These are tests organized by the Superior Council of the Judiciary, which also includes training provided by the Judicial School of Colombia.

Candidates who pass the examination are then included on eligibility lists and are finally appointed, in the case of trial judges, by the plenary assembly of district courts and, for magistrates composing these courts, by the Supreme Court of Justice (for ordinary judicial jurisdiction), by the Council of State (for administrative contentious jurisdiction), or by the National Commission of Judicial Discipline (for disciplinary jurisdiction following the entry into force of the constitutional amendment of 2015).

Regarding magistrates of Colombian high courts, it is necessary to distinguish between the nomination procedures for members of the Constitutional Court and those provided in the 1991 Constitution (following the constitutional revision of 2015) for members of the Council of State and the Supreme Court of Justice. The latter are appointed by co-option, as it is the plenary assemblies of these bodies that select them from a list of candidates prepared by the Superior Council of the Judiciary. As for the magistrates of the Constitutional Court, they are appointed externally by the Senate of the Republic, upon proposal of the President of the Republic, the Council of State, and the Supreme Court, with each of these actors proposing one-third of the members.

2. CLERKS OF COURT

In Colombia, there is no legal actor similar to a court clerk, nor, in a broader sense, an institution of court clerking as known in France and other countries. Therefore, in the absence of such a reference, we will here discuss judicial office employees (*empleados de despachos judiciales*).

The Colombian Law on the Administration of Justice of 1996 provides that every judicial office must have a support and assistance team for the work of the judge or magistrate, composed of employees from the judicial career, belonging to administrative, professional, technical, and operational levels. Although the law on the administration of justice states that the Superior Council of the Judiciary is the authority that determines the personnel structure serving judges and magistrates, the same law stipulates that in every judicial office, a minimum structure must be ensured, consisting of at least three employees. Specifically, each office must have a secretary, a judicial assistant, and an auxiliary.

The secretary of the judicial office is responsible for handling the files concerning all cases brought before the judges or magistrates. This includes all communications to the parties and interveners during a proceeding and daily reporting to the office holder on the status of each procedure, as well as the office's statistics. The judicial assistant (*asesor*, *sustanciador*, or *oficial mayor*) is responsible for studying, drafting, and preparing all documents that the judge or magistrate must sign in the context of a given procedure. Finally, the office auxiliary carries out tasks such as executing orders from the judge or magistrate, including notifications and summonses. They also ensure the execution of administrative orders directly given by the office's secretary.

According to the Colombian Law on the Administration of Justice, all judicial office employees are career civil servants recruited through a public competition. This competition is organized by the Superior Council of the Judiciary, from which lists of eligible candidates are established.

Based on these lists, the various judicial office employees are directly appointed by the judge or magistrate in charge of the respective judicial office.

3. LAWYERS

Unlike the French legal system and many other national systems, Colombian law regarding the legal profession, dating back to 1971, stipulates that university studies undertaken at law faculties (whether public or private) always and exclusively lead to the title of lawyer. In other words, all law students, upon completing five years of education, become lawyers.

Initially, it is the law faculty within each university institution that awards the lawyer's degree to students who have passed the five final exams, known as preparatory exams, and who have also successfully defended a final thesis or, instead of writing and defending a thesis, have completed a nine to twelve-month internship (*judicatura*) in a judicial office, administrative authority, or law firm.

Subsequently, upon obtaining the lawyer's degree and possessing the certificates of completion, thesis defense, or internship completion, the student must apply to the Public Registry of Lawyers, an administrative unit of the Superior Council of the Judiciary, to obtain a professional lawyer's card. This card is the actual credential allowing lawyers to practice their profession in Colombia.

Lawyers are not organized into bar associations, as such an institution does not exist. It is sufficient to hold the professional lawyer's card, valid indefinitely, and not be suspended or struck off following a disciplinary legal procedure, to offer all the services of a lawyer throughout Colombian territory. However, it is important to note that not all those who successfully complete their law studies formally become lawyers (that is the title and the diploma upon completion), nor can it be considered, substantively, that they all practice the profession of lawyer.

Thus, a Colombian lawyer may become a state official, a contractual employee of the state, a judge or magistrate, a notary, or a corporate legal counsel. Therefore, the only lawyers who truly work as lawyers are those who are part of a legal council, those who provide representation to others to conclude legal acts or contracts, and those who plead before judicial or administrative authorities. These lawyers work either independently, in small firms (boutiques), or in large national or international firms.

Both advisory and representation activities, as well as those related to advocacy, must all be conducted in accordance with Law 1123 of 2007, the Lawyer's Disciplinary Code. Even though the constitutional revision of 2015 opens the door to a possible creation of bar associations and the exercise of disciplinary powers within each bar association, the National Commission on Judicial

Discipline remains responsible for disciplinary action against lawyers in Colombia.

4. NOTARIES

Notaries are individuals authorized to provide the public service of notarization. That's why they are considered authorities and are subject to the civil, disciplinary, and criminal liability system of public officials.

The main areas of intervention of notaries in Colombia are, succinctly, as follows: (1) producing documents with the force of an official document (*escrituras públicas*) as solemn legal acts reflecting the expression of the will of one or more persons; (2) certifying the authenticity of a private document or the signature of individuals or officials (*reconocimiento*); (3) certifying the authenticity of copies of public or private documents (*autenticación*); (4) preserving the deposit of deeds or any kind of document in their original version (*protocolización*); (5) authorizing and preserving wills; (6) establishing and maintaining the registry of the civil status of individuals and certifying it (*registro civil*).

As for the method of appointment of notaries in Colombia, the Notary Law of 1970 stipulates that the Superior Council of the Notarial Career must organize a public competition, with the participation of the Ministry of Justice and the High Authority of Notary and Public Registry (*Superintendencia de Notariado y Registro*). This competition must include the evaluation of the candidate's dossier, interviews, and specialized knowledge and public administration tests.

Following the competition, the national government must appoint the candidates with the highest results as titular notaries (*notario en propiedad*) in circuits where there are positions to be filled. The titular notary performs his functions until he reaches the mandatory retirement age. However, in the event that there are positions to be filled but no definitive result from a given competition yet, the government can appoint, based on the dossier, an interim notary (*notario interino*). Finally, the Notary Law stipulates that in the case of temporary absence of the titular notary, he or she appoints a provisional notary (*notario encargado*), whose selection must then be ratified by the mayor of the city.

5. BAILIFFS

In Colombia, there isn't an exact equivalent to the judicial officer known as a court bailiff in France and other countries. However, there exists another category of legal professionals in Colombia, namely auxiliary officers of justice (*auxiliares de la justicia*), which should be studied in terms of the equivalence of functions, often used in legal comparisons.

According to the General Code of Procedure adopted in 2012, auxiliary officers of justice are individuals who perform a transient public function within a specific case due to their expertise and specialized knowledge in certain areas. They intervene during legal proceedings to carry out various types of tasks. Often, they are appointed as temporary administrators of movable or immovable property (*sequestrators*) that have been previously seized. Additionally, other auxiliary officers of justice may be appointed to fulfill various functions such as accounting agents, liquidators, responsible for inheritance division, interpreters, or translators. Their involvement in a legal case allows them to earn fees for the work duly performed.

To become an auxiliary officer of justice, one simply needs to register on a list of auxiliary officers of justice, administered either by the Superior Council of the Judiciary or by each trial judge, court, or high court. Subsequently, it is the judge or magistrate who, in practice, will appoint them as auxiliary officers of justice. This is a function that cannot be refused or waived, except in certain cases stipulated by Colombian law.

6. CORPORATE LAWYERS

In Colombia, in-house lawyers are simply attorneys who have chosen to be employed within a company. This mainly involves large companies that recruit these lawyers to join their own legal department, but it is also possible for medium-sized companies to hire a single lawyer with versatile functions. Moreover, neither the law nor regulations provide special oversight for this activity. Therefore, the skills and the recruitment methods of in-house lawyers are governed by market laws, the policies of each company, and the content of the contracts (employment or service agreements) expressly signed between the lawyer and the company.

In any case, it is customary in Colombia for in-house lawyers to provide daily advice in areas of private law, particularly in property and contract law, and business law (especially regarding commercial property and contracts, commercial companies, and market law).

As a result, it is rare (though not impossible) for an in-house lawyer to provide permanent legal advice in fields such as labor law or tax law, which is often handled by law firms that act as consultants for companies.

Similarly, in most cases, in-house lawyers, although formally attorneys, do not include among their duties the representation of the company before Colombian judicial authorities. Business law litigation, as well as any other type of litigation, is typically handled through specialized law firms or so-called "external" lawyers, as opposed to "internal" in-house lawyers.

CHAPTER FIVE

CRIMINAL LAW

Colombian criminal law originates from the continental European tradition, with significant influence particularly from German and Spanish law. The current legislation, the Penal Code of 2000, replaced the Penal Code of 1980, which was characterized by a marked neoclassical causalist trend and had repealed the punitive statute of 1936, inspired by Italian positivism. The drafters of the 2000 Penal Code explicitly stated that they did not adopt any specific theoretical framework, thus allowing the dynamics of case law to progressively shape the orientation of the Colombian penal system.

1. SUBSTANTIVE CRIMINAL LAW

In conceptualizing punishable conduct, Colombian legislation acknowledges the traditional distinction between felonies (more serious behaviors adjudicated by the judiciary) and misdemeanors (minor offenses warranting administrative sanctions). Additionally, the legislation (Penal Code, art. 9) includes the categories of typicity, unlawfulness, and culpability, emphasizing that "causality alone is not sufficient for the legal imputation of the result." The notion of crime as a social phenomenon prevails over the dogma of causality in criminal behaviors and the idea of crime as a natural fact.

The idea of not adhering to any particular theoretical framework materializes in several aspects of the statute. For example, the reference to objective imputation opens the door to functionalist theses without committing to any specific one. Similarly, regarding the position of guarantor, its statements are not confined to a particular theoretical model. The causes for the exclusion of criminal responsibility are stated in general terms (Penal Code, art. 32), without specifying whether they pertain to the absence of typicity, justification, or non-culpability.

Regarding direct action and participation, the Colombian penal system retains the traditional notions of individual perpetrator (sole perpetrator), multiple perpetrators (co-perpetrators or indirect perpetrators), and participants (accomplices and instigators or determiners). The innovation lies in the categories of intervenors and individuals acting on behalf of others. Initially, an "intervenor" was considered a person participating in a crime with a qualified active subject (Penal Code, art. 30, final paragraph); however, contemporary jurisprudence assigns them direct responsibility. An intervenor is an unqualified subject—extraneus—who performs the conduct described in the offense prescribed by law, for a qualified active subject—intraneus. Thus, for qualified special offenses, Colombian criminal law allows the application of the same penal norm to those who co-act in what is contrary to criminal law, regardless of the conditions required for the qualified perpetrator.

Moreover, acting on behalf of another (Penal Code, art. 29, para. 3) has been incorporated into the current legislation as a formula to address punishable conduct materializing in actions of corporate entities. Although Colombian criminal law does not exclude the possibility of imputing criminal responsibility to legal entities, this possibility has not yet materialized. The hypothesis of an act performed for another allows natural persons fulfilling a particular function assigned to a legal entity to assume the criminal responsibilities resulting from illegal actions. An example is the "omission by a withholding agent," which occurs when the legal entity collecting the value-added tax (VAT) fails to remit the collected sums to the tax authority within the legally stipulated deadlines; in such cases, it is understood that the natural persons responsible for this obligation act on behalf of the legal entity and, consequently, assume the criminal responsibility.

In the case of associating punishable conduct, the exclusion of arithmetic addition of sentences is maintained, opting traditionally for the legal sum. A person guilty of more than two punishable behaviors is subject to a single sentence, which cannot exceed the arithmetic sum of the penalties for each offense, but is calculated by doubling the penalty provided by law for the most serious offense. Somewhat confusingly, complex offenses and continuous crimes are assimilated to associations of punishable conduct; however, the applicable penalty is less than that provided for their combination.

Culpability is analyzed according to the norms of the finalistic theory (imputability, actualizable awareness of unlawfulness, and the requirement of an alternative conduct), but with nuances peculiar to functionalism. In this regard, jurisprudence has developed very particular notions, combining elements of various crime theories.

As for penalties, the legislation revolves around custodial sentences and pecuniary penalties. The very particular circumstances experienced by Colombia at the end of the 20th century led to a progressive increase in custodial sentences, proportionally much higher than those in other countries. Colombian criminal policy has oscillated between maximalist criteria, tending to apply custodial sentences to as many punishable behaviors as possible, and alternative criteria, recognizing the empirical inefficiency of this approach. The Penal Code of 2000 opened up a broad framework for applying pecuniary penalties and alternative mechanisms to imprisonment, which, however, have so far been neglected in judicial practice.

Regarding special criminal law, the current legislation is characterized by a significant increase in the catalog of offenses, due to several reasons: (1) during the last three decades of the 20th century, specialized statutes regulating offenses outside the Penal Code proliferated; indeed, one of the main objectives of the 2000 penal legislation was to recodify into a single statute all offenses previously dispersed across a multitude of specialized norms; (2) international criminal law provisions were included in the Penal Code pursuant to commitments made by ratifying international treaties; (3) behaviors arising from new technologies and contemporary trends in transnational crime were cataloged.

Regarding legislative technique, broad descriptions and extended modalities are preferred, allowing greater interpretative latitude. In accordance with international norms, the number of offenses with an "abstract risk" has also increased, and the protection of legal goods has been anticipated. Concurrently, a process of decriminalizing socially innocuous behaviors has begun.

2. CRIMINAL PROCEDURE

In Colombia, since 1 January 2005, two procedural systems coexist.

The first is an inquisitorial system, designed based on the principles established by the 1991 Constitution, wherein the prosecution is responsible for directing and initiating criminal investigations, except for offenses under the jurisdiction of military criminal justice, which covers their subjects. Once the investigation and evidence collection are established, the prosecution decides whether to dismiss the investigation due to lack of sufficient evidence or to prosecute, in which case a judicial decision of indictment is issued, and the trial phase begins before a judge, who conducts the corresponding public hearing and renders the verdict. The sentence execution phase is entrusted to another judge called the "judge of execution of sentences and security measures."

The characteristics of this procedural system, applicable to crimes committed before 1 January 2005, are as follows:

- *Judicial and Jurisdictional Functions*: The prosecution investigates, instructs, and qualifies. This means it acts as a genuine investigating judge, inherent to the inquisitorial system, collecting evidence and validly incorporating it into the trial (principle of evidence permanence), before evaluating it to determine if there is a sufficient evidentiary basis to guarantee fundamental rights during the trial (conservatory measures, safeguard measures, etc.). Finally, it also examines whether there is a foundation for prosecution, issuing a judicial order containing the accusation and evaluating the provided evidence.

- *Principle of Judicial Information and Obligation*: The exercise of action is guided by the principle of mandatory definition and occurs when the prosecution issues the indictment resolution. This means that in this process, the possibility of applying the principle of opportunity is excluded.
- *Absence of External Judicial Control over Prosecution's Actions*: The prosecution belongs to the judicial branch, makes judicial decisions, and is vested with judicial powers; therefore, during the investigation phase, there is no form of control over its actions, except for the possibility of requesting a judge to control the legality of security measures or decisions related to property. However, in such cases, the judge is limited by the evaluation of evidence, which is under the prosecutor's jurisdiction. Neither the foreclosure nor the accusation is subject to judicial control.
- *Exercise of the Right of Contradiction before the Judge*: The accused exercises their right of contradiction before the prosecutor and the judge, both vested with judicial functions, meaning they are both counterparts, decide on the requests made by the accused, and evaluate the evidence.
- *Principle of Judicial Information in Evidence Matters*: Although the prosecution and the defense may request

evidence, the judge can also order its practice to clarify the truth.
- *Mechanisms of Flexibility*: There are forms of early closure of the procedure allowing, in certain cases, to terminate the criminal action and, among other things, to obtain convictions without trial, following an acceptance of charges by the accused.

The other procedural system, in force in Colombia for crimes committed since 1 January 2005, is accusatory and presents distinct characteristics, namely:

- *Jurisdictional and Non-Judicial Function*: The prosecution retains its investigative functions and its belonging to the jurisdictional branch of public power but is stripped of its instructional functions and judicial powers affecting fundamental rights. This is because, on the one hand, the principle of concentration of evidence is in force, whereby evidence is established in the trial, and, on the other hand, the guarantee of fundamental rights falls under the competence of a new judge, called the "judge of guarantees."
- *Principle of Judicial Information and Mandatory Definition, with Exceptional Admission of the Principle of Opportunity*: The general rule of judicial information and mandatory definition is maintained, but it is admitted that the prosecution, exceptionally, can apply the principle of opportunity for reasons of criminal policy, in cases expressly authorized by the legislator and with judicial control of legality by the judge of guarantees.
- *External Control by the Judge of Guarantees*: The general rule is that the infringement of fundamental rights is under the jurisdiction of the judge of guarantees (conservatory measures, safeguard measures, etc.). However, in some cases, depending on the degree of infringement of

the fundamental right and its hierarchy, the prosecution is authorized to conduct proceedings autonomously and, among other things, subject to prior or subsequent control by the judge of guarantees, according to the legal definition, based on the fundamental right at stake.

- *Exercise of the Right of Contradiction*: The accused can exercise the right of contradiction and request the production of evidence from the judge and the prosecution, who evaluate and decide on them.
- *Dispositive Principle in Evidence Matters*: The judge cannot order the search for evidence *ex officio*; therefore, the burden of proof lies with the parties.
- *Mechanisms of Flexibility*: Besides the mechanisms of extinguishing the criminal action and early termination of the procedure, as established in the previous system, the principle of opportunity is introduced, as well as pre-agreements or negotiations between the accused and the prosecution, as mechanisms to ease the exercise of criminal action.

CHAPTER SIX

PERSONS

In civil law, we are persons: human beings, individuals, men, women, etc. However, not all persons recognized by civil law are human beings.

In the legal realm, there are two categories of persons, two kinds of legal subjects: natural persons and legal persons. Both are endowed with legal personality and, consequently, holders of personal rights.

1. DISTINCTION BETWEEN NATURAL AND JURIDICAL PERSONS

Article 73 of the Civil Code establishes that there are natural and legal persons. The code then continues to outline, among other things, the rules regarding the beginning and end of legal personality, civil status, and capacity.

Regarding natural persons, articles 90 and following of the Civil Code outline the rules related to the beginning and end of legal personality.

The personality of a natural person begins at birth. Article 90 of the Civil Code sets the conditions for the birth of a human being:

- Total separation from the mother is essential; some authors have stated that it is necessary to cut the umbilical cord;
- The human being must have lived after separation; this establishes the "theory of vitality" and not the "theory of

viability." Therefore, it is necessary to prove that the person lived, at least for an instant;

- The Code specifically requires that the newborn is a human being. In Colombian law, it is the genus that defines who is a human being.

Every birth must be registered in the civil status register, which must include the identity of the mother, the day, and the hour of birth.

Regarding the condition of the unborn child (*nasciturus*), Colombian law considers it a portion or part of the mother, in the same sense it was conceived in Roman law. However, the Civil Code, in its articles 91 and 93, provides for the protection of the unborn child. Consequently, the judge must take decisions to protect the existence of the unborn child.

Article 122 of the Colombian Penal Code equates the interruption of pregnancy with a crime. However, ruling C-355 of 10 May 2006, issued by the Constitutional Court, highlighted three possible exemptions, primarily considering risks to the mother's health.

According to article 94 of the Civil Code, the personality of a natural person ends with their death. Article 2 of Decree 1546 of 1998 establishes that the life of a human person ends with "brain death," defined as the biological phenomenon occurring when the absence of brainstem functions is irreversibly verified. Brain death requires the presence of these seven signs: absence of spontaneous respiration, dilated pupils, absence of pupillary reflex, absence of corneal reflex, absence of vestibular-ocular reflex, absence of gag reflex, and absence of cough reflex.

The death of a natural person can be real or presumed. Articles 96 to 109 of the Colombian Civil Code regulate the presumption of death due to the disappearance of the natural person.

Concerning the beginning and end of the legal personality of legal persons, it should first be mentioned that legal persons can be public or private.

Article 633 of the Civil Code states that private law legal persons are of two types: corporations or associations, and foundations. Corporations or associations are created to satisfy the interests of the associates. In contrast, in foundations, the founder creates the legal person to satisfy a general interest.

For the creation of a legal person, three essential conditions must be met: a constitutive legal act, state authorization for certain groups of persons, and the organization itself.

First, it is essential to conclude a legal act by which the parties create a legal person different from the associates. Regarding associations, article 98 of the Commercial Code states that the "partnership agreement" is the agreement by which two or more people commit to making certain contributions in money, labor, or assets valuable in monetary terms, with the aim of sharing the profits obtained among them. In contrast, for the creation of a foundation, only the founder's declaration of intent regarding the formation, functioning, and necessary statutes for the foundation's life is needed.

Second, for the creation of certain legal persons—churches, religious organizations, associations of ministers, among others—the law requires state authorization. However, in general, the creation of private law legal persons does not depend on state authorization. Instead, they are created by the mere agreement of wills.

Finally, the organization of the legal person is required, by establishing rules governing the internal and external life of the legal subject. This set of rules must address the name, domicile, social purpose, contributions of the members, duration, organs, and generally all conditions for the functioning of the legal person. This set of rules constitutes the "statutes" of the legal person.

Concerning the end of the legal person, Colombian law provides several causes of extinction: collective agreement of dissolution, the arrival of the expiration date provided (C. com., art. 218, no. 1), realization of the social purpose (C. com., art. 218, no. 2), death or resignation of one of the associates (C. civ., art. 648).

Recently, the debate on the recognition of legal subjectivity has been opened through jurisprudence.

In ruling T-622 of 10 November 2016, the Colombian Constitutional Court recognized the river Atrato as a subject of rights to guarantee its protection.

Another case is found in the ruling of the Colombian Supreme Court of Justice on 26 July 2017, #AHC48062017, where the Civil Chamber protected the habeas corpus of a bear named "Chucho;" since then, animals are no longer considered mere property at the service of man, but as subjects of utmost importance in an "ecocentric" vision of the law.

These judicial decisions have opened a significant debate on the category of legal subjects in Colombian law, and the debate is not yet closed.

Natural and legal persons enjoy certain "attributes of personality;" among them: name and surname, civil status, patrimony, capacity, domicile, and nationality.

Civil status is determined by law and by all the legal situations in which a natural person finds themselves, relating them to their family or society (C. civ., arts. 396 to 410).

The civil situations and qualities of persons have two main functions: they serve to fully identify individuals and to assign to each their corresponding rights and obligations. In this sense, civil status determines the legal situation of the human person in society and the family; it means that civil status situates the natural person within the State, family, and society.

In Colombian positive law, civil status has the following characteristics:

- Every person has a civil status because, in principle, one can identify in every person their qualities of man or woman, adult or minor, single or married;
- Civil status is indivisible because a person cannot have two contradictory civil statuses;

- The qualities of civil status are absolute because they are enforceable against all;
- The qualities of civil status are not subject to commerce.

Regarding the proof of civil status, it is evidenced by the civil status register, governed by the Civil Status Statute (Decree 1260 of 1970). This norm establishes that all civil status and its modifications must be registered. This registration obligation allows the legislator to establish a formal and unique evidence system. Thus, civil status can only be proven by the specific sheet of the civil status register.

Articles 396 and following of the Civil Code provide rules concerning the possession of civil status. This can be defined as the outward manifestation of civil status; it is the act of behaving towards others as the holder of the possessed civil status. Thus, the prolonged exercise of a particular right presumes its existence. Article 399 of the Civil Code establishes that the possession of civil status can be proven by a set of testimonies.

In general, capacity implies, on the one hand, the aptitude to be a subject of rights, and on the other hand, the aptitude to exercise and defend one's rights. This distinction gives rise to the dualism inherent in the notion of capacity in Colombian law: capacity of rights or enjoyment and capacity to act.

Concerning the capacity of natural persons, the notions of capacity of enjoyment and capacity to act must be distinguished. The capacity of rights or enjoyment of a natural person consists of the ability to be the holder of rights. Every person, regardless of sex or age (for example, a child or a homeless person), has the capacity to hold their civil rights of a patrimonial nature: real rights, credit rights, intangible rights, and hereditary rights.

However, the capacity to exercise a right presupposes the existence of a fully developed will. Thus, a child has the capacity of enjoyment of their rights but not the capacity to exercise them. Consequently, the capacity to act is linked to the existence of a reflective will. In this sense, Colombian law grants the capacity to act to any person over 18 years old (Law 27 of 1977). Political capacity, on the other hand, is linked to the capacity to act but is reserved only for Colombian nationals.

Article 1503 of the Civil Code prescribes the presumption of capacity, establishing that every person is capable, except for those whom the law has expressly declared incapable.

Regarding the capacity of legal persons, article 633 of the Civil Code establishes that the latter is a fictitious person, with the capacity to exercise rights and have obligations. Thus, in matters of legal persons, it is also necessary to distinguish the capacities of enjoyment and of exercise. First, it should be noted that the capacity of enjoyment of the legal person begins at the moment it comes into legal existence.

According to Law 57 of 1887, legal persons can acquire all types of assets and can be holders of real rights: property, usufruct, servitude, pledge, and mortgage. But the capacity of enjoyment of legal persons is mainly manifested in matters of credit, i.e., personal rights and obligations. Concerning intangible rights, copyright, and industrial property, they are of great importance for legal persons, more so than for natural persons. Finally, legal persons have the capacity of enjoyment of hereditary rights.

Secondly, the capacity of a legal person to exercise its rights is developed through the contract as a vehicle of its will. Legal persons have the capacity to exercise their rights and the capacity to obligate themselves through the contract. Certainly, the capacity to act of legal.

2. RIGHTS ATTACHED TO PERSONALITY

Natural persons hold several personality rights. Among the fundamental rights of human beings, the right to life, honor, one's own image, the inviolability of the home, respect for private life, and health are generally considered paramount. Additionally, rights such as the right to a name, bodily integrity, and one's own appearance are also considered personality rights.

In contrast, legal entities do not possess most personality rights. The only personality rights recognized for legal entities are the social name and honor. However, this does not prevent legal entities from holding fundamental rights (see judgments T-496 of 1 August 1992, and T-396 of 16 September 1992, of the Colombian Constitutional Court).

Some authors argue that personality rights are not subjective rights because there cannot be rights over the same person; the person would simultaneously be the subject and object of personality rights. Thus, it has been asserted that personality rights are merely legal assets protected by law. However, recent doctrine concerning the legal nature of personality rights affirms that these rights are true subjective rights.

Personality rights are absolute, as their respect is obligatory for all; they belong to a person from birth until death; they are non-transferable and their value cannot be estimated in monetary terms.

The 1991 Colombian Political Constitution enshrines human rights, respect for human dignity, fundamental, social, economic, cultural, and collective rights, and environmental rights, among others. This is the norm that, in Colombian law, enshrines human and personality rights as well as the tools to guarantee them. It is a very generous charter in the enshrinement of personal rights, which has allowed significant progress in the defense of the dignity of Colombians.

Similarly, regarding personality rights in Colombian law, all supranational norms of international law that enshrine these rights are applicable.

CHAPTER SEVEN

THE FAMILY

1. UNIONS

In Colombia, civil marriage was reserved for heterosexual couples since 1887 (C. civ., art. 113) until 2016, the year same-sex marriage was legalized, with the judge being the competent authority to officiate. Since 1988, it has been possible to marry before a notary, and since 1992, the full effects of religious marriage have been recognized, regardless of the religion, as long as it is accepted by the state, whereas previously only Catholic marriages were valid.

Regarding the capacity to enter into this contract, the requirement is to be over 14 years old. Although the law requires parental or legal guardian consent for minors over 14 years old (C. civ., art. 117), the absence of this consent does not affect the marriage contract but constitutes a ground for disinheritance (C. civ., art. 124) and revokes donations already made in favor of the minor (C. civ., art. 125).

As for formalities, two witnesses are required for the celebration of the marriage, unless there is an imminent danger of death. In that case, the marriage contract will only be valid if the death occurs within forty days of the celebration (C. civ., art. 136). The marital system is the marital society, equivalent to the French community property system.

Regarding the grounds for nullity of marriage (C. civ., art. 140), the Constitutional Court has gradually changed the scope of certain provisions. Firstly, concerning the age of the contracting parties, paragraph 2 of article 140 of the Civil Code stipulated that the age limit for men was 14 years and for women 12 years. In 2004, the Court equalized the requirement to 14 years for both future spouses. Concerning violence invoked as a defect of consent, paragraph 5 of the same article equated cohabitation with the ratification of the contract. In 2001, the Court established that the victim of violence could, at any time, demonstrate that the cohabitation was not consensual and request the annulment of the marriage. Regarding abduction (paragraph 6), this was restricted to women only; aiming for equality, the Court extended this to include men. Concerning adultery as a ground for nullity of the marriage contract (paragraph 7), this was declared unconstitutional in 1999. The law (paragraph 8) also opened the way for nullity in cases of murder or assassination, direct or ordered, of the former spouse of one of the two spouses. Since 2003, the Constitutional Court has determined that the nullity of marriage is admissible, if applicable, if both spouses are declared guilty of the crime or if the innocent spouse requests the annulment of the marriage within three months following the final judgment. Finally, before 2003, marriage between an adoptive father and adopted daughter or adoptive mother (or "the former wife of the adoptive father"—paragraph 11) and adopted son was null. The Court has since extended this to include marriages between an adopted daughter and the former husband of the adoptive mother.

The grounds for nullity related to error, incest, or the existence of a previous marriage bond, however, have remained unchanged. Damages may be awarded if the fault of one of the spouses is the cause of the nullity.

By Law 54 of 1990, the Colombian legislator protects unmarried couples, granting civil effects to unions with certain characteristics. The first article of said law states that "from the effective date of this law and for all civil effects concerning it, a *de facto* marital union is one formed by a man and a woman who, without being married, form a permanent and singular community of life." For the union to have legal effects (formation of a "*de facto* patrimonial society" analogous to the marital society of marriage), the partners must not be married and must have lived together for at least two years. Since 2007, the Constitutional Court has extended this union to same-sex couples, as well as to bisexual, transgender, and generally, LGBT community members (Judgment C-075/07). Regarding its dissolution, it is necessary to request judicial division of the society within one year following the separation of the partners or the death of one of the partners. After this period, it is no longer possible to request it in court.

In 2011, the Constitutional Court issued a ruling (C-577/11), declaring the expression "man and woman" in article 113 of the Civil Code constitutional, defining marriage in accordance with Article 42 of the Constitution, which states that the family is the nucleus of society and is formed by a man and a woman. That being said, the Court acknowledged that this was a traditional and narrow interpretation of the family and that a *de facto* marital union was insufficient to guarantee and protect the rights of same-sex couples; therefore, the Court requested Congress to regulate same-sex marriage within two years. In 2013, due to a lack of consensus, the deadline expired; however, the same ruling had stipulated that, in this case, same-sex couples could henceforth celebrate an unnamed contract before a judge or a notary, practically equivalent to civil marriage. Nevertheless, the lack of clarity and more concrete information on the conditions, both substantive and formal, of this contract discouraged its celebration. However, by a historic ruling (SU-214/16 of 28 April 2016), the Constitutional Court opened the way for civil marriage for same-sex couples, thus addressing the protection deficit perpetuated by its 2011 ruling. It is important to note that in Colombia, adoption is not exclusively linked to marriage, which is why the Court's decisions do not concern this institution. It should be emphasized that, by ruling C-683/15, the Constitutional Court recognizes that the notion of family enshrined in the Constitution includes same-sex families, and therefore, same-sex couples have the possibility of adopting a child.

Furthermore, according to Colombian law, it is through the conclusion of marital agreements that future spouses can grant each other mutual donations, without these affecting the rights granted by law to each spouse and their descendants. These donations are irrevocable (C. civ., art. 1463), are conditioned on the celebration of the marriage, and concern present or future assets (C. civ., art. 1771). If it is a donation of future and universal assets, it amounts to an inheritance institution, as marital agreements indirectly involve a succession allocation. The Colombian Civil Code also allows revocable donations between spouses (C. civ., art. 1196), and since donations become irrevocable upon the donor's death (C. civ., art. 1203), this also amounts to a testamentary disposition, devoid of the formalities of a will.

2. DISSOLUTION OF UNIONS

The law provides several grounds for the dissolution of the marital bond, specifically: actual or declared death, and divorce.

The grounds for divorce in Colombian law are as follows (C. civ., art. 154): (1) adultery (in 2000, the Constitutional Court declared unconstitutional the exception to the rule regarding forgiveness or consent by the innocent spouse); (2) serious failure to fulfill the duties imposed by law towards the other spouse or the couple's children; (3) abuse; (4) habitual drunkenness; (5) habitual use of hallucinogenic substances; (6) any serious or incurable disease or abnormality that endangers the physical or mental health of the other spouse; (7) acts of corruption or perversion towards the other spouse, descendants, persons under their care, and living under the same roof; (8) *de facto* or judicial separation for at least two years; (9) mutual agreement of the parties (since 2005, notaries are competent to record this declaration of intent).

3. FILIATION AND PARENTAGE

Regarding filiation, Law 29 of 1982 establishes that all children, whether born within a marriage, conceived out of wedlock, or adopted, enjoy the same rights and obligations. The establishment of filiation for a child born to a married couple or a common-law couple benefits from a presumption of fact. Paternity or maternity can be contested by the spouse, permanent partner, and mother within 140 days of discovering the non-biological paternity or maternity.

The child can also contest paternity or maternity without any time constraint.

In 2006, the Colombian legislature modernized the adoption regim established by the Civil Code. Currently, adoption is regulated in the Code of Childhood and Adolescence (Law 1069 of 2006, articles 60 to 78). It is stipulated that individuals over 25 years old and at least 15 years older than the child to be adopted are eligible for adoption. Thus, single individuals, spouses, permanent partners, guardians, and the spouse or permanent partner of the child's parent can validly apply for adoption. Having existing children is not an obstacle to the application; the procedure is entirely free of charge, and there is a preferential right for Colombian adoptive parents over foreigners. Before 1989, there were only two categories of adoption: simple adoption and full adoption; but since then, only full adoption has persisted, and until 2015, it was reserved for heterosexual couples. On 4 November 2015, the Constitutional Court rendered a constitutionality ruling (C-683/15), considering the best interest of the child, in which it opened adoption to same-sex couples under the same conditions as heterosexual couples.

4. SUCCESSIONS

The Colombian Civil Code establishes that real rights are acquired through one of the modes of acquisition (*modo*). However, this modo must be justified by a named cause, the *título*. This combination legally consolidates the acquisition of real rights. Concerning the real right represented by inheritance, it is acquired by "succession due to death;" the law or the will are the titles that justify this acquisition. Therefore, the law governs the transfer of property when the deceased has made no provision or when it has proved ineffective (C. civ., art. 1037). Consequently, a person's succession can be entirely legal, entirely testamentary, partially legal, or partially testamentary (C. civ., art. 1009). Succession due to death, as a means of acquiring the transferable rights of the deceased, is complex, as it involves three phases: the death of the decedent (*de cujus*), the hereditary vocation, and the acceptance of the inheritance, technically consisting of renouncing the refusal of it, as the heir has legal possession (C. civ., art. 783).

In general, the Colombian Civil Code constructs the succession regime on hereditary vocation, either by blood or civil relations, although there are two exceptional situations where the persons called to succeed have no such relationship with the decedent. According to article 1040 of the Civil Code, the hereditary vocation belongs to the descendants of the deceased, their ascendants, their privileged collaterals, their children, the surviving spouse (Colombian law determines that there is no kinship between spouses), and lastly, the Colombian Family Welfare Institute (ICBF).

In a direct line, descending or ascending, the hereditary vocation is not limited; but lower degrees exclude others, without prejudice to the right of hereditary representation (C. civ., arts. 1040, 1041, 1042, 1043, 1045, and 1046). In the collateral line, the hereditary vocation corresponds to second-degree relatives and, failing that, to third-degree relatives, only if they are the deceased's nephews (C. civ., arts. 1047 and 1051). Hereditary representation also occurs for the benefit of the descendants of the deceased's siblings (C. civ., art. 1043).

The Colombian Civil Code specifies that the deceased's legal heirs must be alive at the time of death (C. civ., art. 1019), implying the capacity to enjoy rights. That said, the same code allows for a provision in favor of someone not yet alive at the time of the deceased's death, as an executory condition, within ten years following the opening of the succession (C. civ., art. 1019). Similarly, it is possible to make a provision to a person in gratitude for a significant service, even if that person did not exist at the testator's death (C. civ., art. 1019). Exceptionally, a provision can also be made for the future creation of a corporation or establishment (C. civ., art. 1020).

In Colombia, minors over 14 years old can validly draft a will (C. civ., art. 1060); however, they must have the capacity to exercise other legal acts with succession implications, such as donations to legitimate heirs or the reserve to improve descendants' situations (*mejoras*).

Concerning intestate or legal succession, the Civil Code specifies that gender or being the family's eldest does not impact and gives no privilege (C. civ., art. 1039). Likewise, it grants equal inheritance rights to foreigners compared to nationals (C. civ., arts. 1053 and 1054).

Notably, the Colombian Civil Code, in regulating legal succession, does not consider the origin of the assets (C. civ., art. 1038); in other words, Colombian law does not recognize cases where, due to the assets' origin, they must be returned to a certain person upon the owner's death, or, equivalently, abnormal successions do not exist.

Regarding the surviving spouse, they can request, in the division of the inheritance, the share corresponding to the common property, called gananciales, as well as the marital portion intended exclusively for those without the financial means to adequately meet their needs. But they can also inherit as they are in the second and third order of succession. By ruling C-283/11, the Constitutional Court affirmed that couples forming a *de facto* marital union had the right to a marital portion, whether heterosexual or homosexual. Similarly, ruling C-238/12 determined that they had mutual hereditary vocation.

Regarding the will, the law defines it as the legal act capable of transmitting assets due to death and generally prohibits contracts related to a succession that has not yet been opened (C. civ., art.

1520). However, exceptionally, the law allows the conclusion of certain contracts involving, directly or indirectly, inheritance allocations, such as the promise to reserve to improve descendants' situations (*mejoras*), inter-spousal donations (C. civ., arts. 1056 and 1196), donations made to a legitimate heir (C. civ., art. 1256), the partition of inheritance by an act inter vivos (C. civ., art. 1375), and the mandate, which must be fulfilled after the principal's death (C. civ., art. 2195).

The will is always a solemn act, but today, under certain circumstances for the testator, it can be concluded without all the solemnities normally required by law; hence, the will is defined as a "more or less" solemn act (C. civ., art. 1064).

The Civil Code classifies wills from the most solemn (open or nuncupative will and closed will—C. civ., art. 1064) to the least solemn or special (verbal, military, and maritime wills—C. civ., art. 1087). The nuncupative and closed wills are formed by notarial act, while privileged wills are valid if established in writing at the testator's death (C. civ., arts. 1070, 1093, 1099, 1103, and 1105).

In Colombian law, there are so-called forced assignments; that is, provisions the testator is legally obliged to apply (C. civ., art. 1226). Until 2018, these forced assignments were: the alimony owed by the testator to certain persons by law, the marital portion, a reserve called legitimate, and a reserve called *mejoras* (C. civ., art. 1226). The legitimate reserve corresponded to the portion of the deceased's assets intended, by law, for the legitimate heirs—*legitimarios*—(C. civ., art. 1239), that is, their descendants and ascendants (C. civ., art. 1240). The *mejoras* reserve corresponded to the part of the assets obligatorily intended to improve the situation of one, several, or all descendants (C. civ., art. 1242). Thus, the testator could freely dispose of only the remaining quarter (C. civ., art. 1242). The *mejoras* reserve disappeared with Law 1934 of 2018, allowing the testator to freely dispose of 50% of their estate, thus aligning their situation with that of a testator without descendants or ascendants, who also has full freedom to dispose of half of their assets.

CHAPTER EIGHT

PROPERTY

1. SCOPE OF PROPERTY

Tangible property can be perceived by the senses, while intangible property can only be perceived by the mind. The latter includes personal and real rights.

Tangible property can be either immovable or movable (C. civ., art. 655).

Movable property is capable of being moved. There are two categories:

- *Movable property by nature* (C. civ., art. 655): These are items that can move by themselves or be moved by an external force.
- *Movable property by anticipation* (C. civ., art. 659): These are immovable items considered by law to be movable in view of their imminent state.

Immovable property consists of items that cannot change place or are considered immovable by legal fiction, even though they are naturally movable:

- *Immovable property by nature*: These items cannot be moved without altering their substance.
- *Immovable property by adhesion*: These are naturally movable items that are permanently and materially

incorporated into an immovable property. In this case, the law considers them immovable.
- *Immovable property by destination*: These are naturally movable items considered immovable by law because the owner has attached them to the service of an estate.

In Colombia, the Civil Code establishes that intangible things are mere rights, such as personal rights, real rights, or active easements (C. civ., art. 653). Colombian doctrine has criticized this article on the grounds that some rights are not patrimonial, such as political rights. In this sense, not all rights can be considered intangible property, as a property can be part of the patrimony.

There are rights to intangible property, such as intellectual property that protects copyright, and industrial property.

According to Andean Decision 351 of 1993, copyright protects literary works, lectures, musical creations, theatrical and musical theater pieces, choreographies and pantomimes, cinematographic and audiovisual works, graphic and plastic art works, architectural works, photographic works, applied art creations, illustrations, maps, plans, sketches, drafts, software, anthologies, and databases that constitute personal creations.

New creations and distinctive signs are protected by industrial property through Andean Decision 486. Among new creations are invention patents, utility models, trade secrets, industrial designs, and integrated circuit layout designs. Among distinctive signs, the standard protects commercial slogans, trademarks, collective marks, certification marks, trade names, trade signs, geographical indications, designations of origin, indications of source, and well-known distinctive signs.

2. POWERS OVER THINGS

The Civil Code states that a real right is one held over a thing, without regard to a specific person (C. civ., art. 665). According to the law, real rights include: the right of ownership, the right of inheritance, the right of usufruct, the right of use and habitation, the right of active servitude, the right of pledge, and the right of mortgage.

Real rights can be principal or accessory. Principal real rights are considered to have their own legal existence and do not guarantee the existence of other rights, such as ownership, usufruct, use, and habitation. Accessory real rights depend on another right for their existence, like mortgages, pledges, and servitudes.

The prerogatives of real rights include the right of pursuit and the right of preference.

The right of pursuit allows the exercise of a right over one's property, regardless of whose hands it is in. This prerogative permits recovery of the property through various actions, such as possessory action, action in revendication, and mortgage action.

The right of preference grants the holder the right to priority payment, allowing them to exclude anyone with only a credit right or a subsequent real right.

According to the Civil Code, possession is the factual relationship between a person and a thing, with the intent of owning it: one must have the intention to possess the thing and the sense of being its owner (C. civ., art. 762). The elements characterizing possession are corpus and animus.

Corpus is the factual control over the thing, but it does not mean the person must have physical contact with the thing (one can possess property even if it is kept away from them).

Animus is the psychological or intellectual element of possession: it involves the intent to act as owner and master over the thing.

By law, possession in Colombia is not a right but a fact. Even though the law protects this fact through judicial actions, possession cannot be assigned or transferred, as it is not a right.

According to article 762 of the Civil Code, the possessor is presumed to be the owner until proven otherwise. This presumption applies to all possessors, whether in good or bad faith, regular or irregular. Possession can lead to acquiring ownership by usucapion, thus consolidating the factual situation. The publician action is granted to the regular possessor to reclaim the property they possessed (C. civ., art. 951). This action cannot be used against the owner. For immovable property, there are possessory actions (C. civ., art. 972).

According to the law, a possessor in bad faith is obliged to restore the natural and civil fruits of the thing, not only those received but also those the owner would have received with average intelligence if they had possessed the thing (C. civ., art. 964).

A possessor in good faith is not obliged to return the fruits harvested before responding to the claim. However, for the fruits received after the claim, the effects are the same as if they were in bad faith.

Regular possession must be in good faith and originate from a just title, even if the good faith does not persist after possession begins (C. civ., art. 764). In this case, the possessor is not obliged to return the fruits received before the revendicative action. The ordinary acquisitive prescription is three years for movable property and five years for immovable property. The just title is the valid and sufficient legal act to transfer the real right. Good faith is the belief that one has acquired the property by legitimate means, without fraud or any other vice.

Irregular possession is possession without just title, without good faith, or both (C. civ., art. 770). The extraordinary acquisitive prescription is ten years for both movable and immovable property.

Violent possession is acquired by force, which can be current or imminent (C. civ., art. 772). Anyone who has suffered violent possession can act through an anti-pillage action (C. civ., art. 984).

Clandestine possession is acquired secretly, without any outward manifestation, which can be opposed (C. civ., art. 774).

By law, violent and clandestine possessions are considered vitiated, and thus, should not lead to acquisitive prescription. However, the Supreme Court of Justice has established that they can still benefit from extraordinary acquisitive prescription.

Possession can be maintained even if the property is rented, pledged, etc. (C. civ., art. 782). One can lose possession of the thing if it is lost and someone else wants to own it. Possession is also lost if the possessor abandons the thing; however, possession is maintained if the possessor accidentally does not know its location (C. civ., art. 788).

A possessor who legally regains possession of the thing is deemed to have had it throughout the intermediate period (C. civ., art. 792).

3. USE OF PROPERTY FOR PURPOSES OF SECURITY

Mortgage is included among the real rights of the Civil Code (C. civ., art. 665); it is a right of pledge on immovable property, which continues under the power of the debtor (C. civ., art. 2432). However, if the obligation to secure the debt is not fulfilled, the holder of the mortgage can request the sale of the property to pay off the credit. In Colombia, it is considered that even if there is no physical control over the property, there exists a legal power of a real nature. For this reason, the mortgage is considered a real right.

Pledge is a real right (C. civ., art. 665) whose security is based on movable property.

Law 1676 of 2013 unified the system of movable guarantees in Colombia. According to this law, a movable guarantee is any transaction that serves to secure an obligation with movable property of the guarantor. Movable guarantees can be established through contracts, which are not accessory but principal, marking a significant change (strongly criticized by legal doctrine), as traditionally these contracts were considered accessory.

4. DISPOSITION OF THINGS

In Colombia, the general rule is the freedom of disposition of property. Nevertheless, real rights cannot be acquired by mere title and mode.

The title is not sufficient to transfer a real right; the title creates obligations, just like a contract. Under Colombian law, the sale contract is a source of obligations, but it does not transfer ownership of the property. The creation of an obligation is different from its fulfillment; the sale contract is only the title, and the mode of acquisition is also needed to transfer ownership. The mode is tradition. For instance, in the case of immovable property, it is necessary, for the tradition, to register the contract at the public instruments office.

CHAPTER NINE

CONTRACT

The contract is conceived as an instrument inherited from Roman law, which must, however, be adapted according to the philosophical and economic trends of the given era. Indeed, it is an essential tool for the fluidity of legal relationships and commercial transactions. The Colombian Civil Code establishes the general rules for the formation, validity, and execution of private contracts. However, to study contracts, it is also necessary to review the specificities of administrative contracts.

1. CONTRACT IN PRIVATE LAW

The private law contract is one of the sources of obligations, according to article 1494 of the Civil Code, and consists of the agreement of wills intended to produce legal effects. It is therefore relevant to study its rules of formation and execution under Colombian law.

1.1. FORMATION

Article 1495 of the Colombian Civil Code defines the contract. It establishes that the contract, or agreement, is an act by which one party undertakes towards another to give, do, or not do something.

The Colombian Civil Code is silent regarding the formation of the contract. The general regime established for the formation of the contract and consent is set out in articles 1502 and following of the Civil Code, as well as in Chapter III, Title I of Book IV of the Commercial Code. These articles prescribe the conditions for obligation: the capacity of the person undertaking the obligation (C. civ., arts. 1503 to 1507), their consent free from defects (C. civ., arts. 1508 to 1516), lawful object (C. civ., arts. 1517 to 1523), and lawful cause (C. civ., arts. 1524 to 1526).

Thus, every contract arises from the agreement of wills; will is the very substance of the contract. For this purpose, the will must be externalized, as unexpressed intentions are not relevant to the law.

Regarding formalism to express will, Colombian law establishes the principle of consensualism, which implies that parties are free to choose the form to express their consent. Exceptionally, the law or agreement of wills may require a specific form for the manifestation of will to conclude a contract (C. civ., art. 1500).

In this sense, the agreement of wills is formed by the meeting of offer and acceptance.

According to article 845 of the Commercial Code, the offer is the proposal to conclude a contract. It must meet certain conditions. Certainly, it must contain all essential elements of the contract; it must be communicated to the recipient by any means (it can be communicated electronically since Law 527 of 1999). Colombian doctrine and the Commercial Code adopt the theory of communication, meaning that it is necessary for the offer to be effectively communicated to the recipient. Thus, the offer has effect only if it has been communicated (Supreme Court of Justice—High Civil Court of Colombian Justice—Civil Cassation, 8 March 1995). Once known by the recipient, the offer is irrevocable (C. com., art. 846).

Regarding acceptance, the Commercial Code does not define it; however, it prescribes its conditions. According to article 854 of the Commercial Code, acceptance is a declaration of will that can be express or implied. If the contract is consensual, once acceptance is sent, it is presumed that the offeror has received it and, consequently, the contract is formed. Conversely, if the contract is solemn, the fulfillment of the prescribed formality is essential (C. civ., arts. 1500 and 1501).

To determine the place of formation of consent, one must observe the rule of article 864 of the Commercial Code. In terms of formation of contracts in electronic commerce, one must observe article 25 of Law 527 of 1999.

Finally, concerning the moment of formation of consent, article 850 of the Commercial Code establishes a rule for verbal contracts between persons present; article 851 of the same code governs the moment of formation of written contracts; and article 523 of Law 527 of 1999 prescribes a specific rule for contracts in electronic commerce.

However, despite the apparent predominance of will in forming the contract under Colombian law, in matters of real rights, the concurrence of two elements is required: the "title" and the "mode." Thus, if the contract concerns a real right, mere consent is not sufficient because the law also requires compliance with the mode provided by law. For example, according to article 740 of the Civil Code, if the contract concerns the transfer of ownership, "tradition" (delivery) is essential for its formation.

1.2. PERFORMANCE AND EXECUTION

Objective good faith was expressly enshrined by the Colombian Civil Code of 1887, following the model of the Chilean code. Article 1603 of this code by Andrés Bello states that "contracts must be executed in good faith." It further adds the phrase "therefore," attributing to good faith a constitutive function in the contractual process, insofar as it must be applied not only to what has been expressly agreed upon, but also to all duties arising "precisely from the nature of the obligation or as prescribed by law." This integration rule is echoed in the Commercial Code of 1971, in its article 871, which adds "with custom and equity." Good faith is expressly required during the pre-contractual period (C. com., art. 863). In 1991, good faith was integrated into positive law at the constitutional level. Article 83 of the Colombian Constitution provides that "the actions of individuals and public authorities must conform to the principles of good faith." Furthermore, there are reiterated instances of this requirement in corporate law, competition law, consumer law, etc. Case law has used good faith as a basis to penalize dishonest maneuvers, which constitute unfair competition, purely formal executions of contracts, omissions from the vigilance duties of the insurer, even in cases of concealment by the insured, or exemption from the performance of essential obligations in contracts. Its scope is such that both case law and doctrine elevate good faith to the level of a general principle, not only in contract law, but also across the entire legal system.

Without an express provision concerning contractual autonomy, manifestations are nonetheless found, which radiate throughout positive law: freedom to conclude a contract and determine its content (C. civ., arts. 1495, 1501 and C. com., art. 864), freedom to choose the form of the contract (C. com., arts. 824 and 826), freedom of form in bilateral promise contracts in commercial law (C. com., art. 861). In parallel, there are limitations: prohibition of abuse of rights (C. com., art. 830), application of the theory of unforeseen circumstances (C. com., art. 868), rescission in case of significant lesion (C. civ., art. 1947). Doctrine and case law have granted the notion the status of a principle.

The binding force of contracts—*pacta sunt servanda*—finds normative consecration in article 1602 of the Civil Code. Regarding the regime of the offer, the Commercial Code, in its article 846, indicates the irrevocability of the offer once communicated, specifying that the offer retains its binding force, including in cases of death or declaration of incapacity of the offeror. Case law and doctrine do not give it the character of a principle, but define the concept as a rule derived from good faith.

A contract produces effects against third parties. In Colombian law, following the model of the French Civil Code, there is an exception to the relative effect of the contract in the promise of representation, also called stipulation for another (*Estipulación en favor de otro*—art. 1506). This stipulation finds practical application in contracts for the transport of goods when the shipper and the recipient are two different subjects, or in franchise contracts when the beneficiary is a person distinct from the franchisor.

Contractual obligations must be fulfilled either upon the term's maturity (determined or determinable), unless the debtor is in default (if, through the debtor's fault, the creditor loses or sees considerably diminished the guarantees constituted in their favor, they have the right to demand performance before maturity), or upon the occurrence of the hypothetical event of the suspensive condition and, in general, after the contract's conclusion. Regarding partial payment, the Civil Code does not specify any concrete provisions; however, some norms grant the creditor the right to the entirety of the performance: "Payment must be made in accordance with the agreed obligation" (C. civ., art. 1627) and "the debtor cannot force the creditor to accept divided performance" (C. civ., art. 1649), unless expressly stated otherwise.

There are exceptions in special law: the drawer of a bill of exchange cannot refuse partial payment (C. com., art. 630), and during commercial bankruptcy proceedings (Law 222/1995, arts. 101, 133 and 198) or personal bankruptcy (General Code of Procedure, art. 540), the creditor must accept debt installment plans. Early payment also does not find concrete regulation on the subject, but when the term benefits exclusively the creditor, the debtor cannot anticipate their performance (C. civ., art. 2251 concerning the deposit contract). Conversely, if the term exclusively benefits the debtor, they can waive it, returning the item early. When the term benefits both parties, the debtor can perform early only if early payment is not prejudicial to the creditor (C. civ., art. 1554). In 1999, to control the fallout of an economic crisis affecting interest rates and home loans, the Colombian legislature obliged banks to accept early payment as well as partial or full payment before term, thereby establishing a kind of favor debitoris (Law 546/1999, art. 17, no. 9), making an exception to the loan rule, which prohibits early payment when interest is contracted (C. com., art. 2229).

The theory of unforeseen circumstances is contemplated by article 868 of the Commercial Code, which provides that "when extraordinary, unforeseen, or unforeseeable circumstances occurring after the conclusion of a contract with successive, periodic, or deferred performance alter or aggravate the future performance that is the responsibility of one of the parties to such a degree that it becomes excessively burdensome, the concerned party may request revision. The judge will then examine the circumstances altering the contract's basis and, if possible, order adjustments according to equity rules. Otherwise, the judge will declare the contract's termination. This rule does not apply to aleatory contracts or contracts with immediate performance." In civil matters, in the absence of an express norm, case law has adopted it since 1936, based on the Roman aphorism *rebus sic stantibus*. It applies in sales contracts, for example, where the buyer's financial status has significantly decreased after contract conclusion, rendering the creditor unable to demand payment (C. com., art. 1882); and in contracts for services and industry (C. Com., art. 2060-2).

Regarding the impossibility of performance, according to the risk theory, two distinct regulations coexist in Colombian positive law. In civil law, the Code assigns the risk of species loss to the buyer (*periculum est emptoris*), unless the debtor is in default of delivery (C. civ., art. 1607). This rule also applies to sales cases (C. civ., art. 1872), but is inapplicable to contracts without property transfer, for which the risk of loss falls on the owner of the item: service contract (C. civ., art. 2059), civil loan (C. civ., art. 2203), mandate (C. civ., art. 2179), and lease (C. civ., art. 2008). Concerning commercial regulation, article 929 of the Commercial Code assigns the risk of loss to the seller (*periculum est venditoris*). Today, case law and the majority doctrine favor extending the commercial rule to civil law.

There is no specific provision in Colombian law defining contractual non-performance, but its contours have been constructed by interpreting rules related to compensating contractual harm; hence, non-performance is analyzed around the debtor's fault. Thus, according to article 1604 of the Civil Code, the debtor is contractually liable when the contract has been totally, imperfectly, or belatedly unperformed, with a prior notice being a prerequisite, except for contracts subject to a deadline (C. civ., art. 1608). Regarding contract termination for non-performance, the Colombian Civil Code follows the French model of tacit resolutory condition in its article 1546 but departs from it in that the judge cannot grant a grace period. The Commercial Code also incorporates this provision, adding a prior requirement of notice (C. com., art. 870). None of the provisions qualify non-performance as resolutory, but case law requires it to be serious, considering the contract's nature, the buyer's interests, or its impact on the contract's economy.

Concerning remedies for non-performance, scattered throughout the general regime in an inconsistent manner, Colombian positive law provides for forced performance in kind (C. civ., art. 1610), the exception of non-performance (C. civ., art. 1609), with uncertain effects, contract resolution, and compensation for contractual harm (C. civ., arts. 1612, 1613 and 1614); *ius variandi* can also be one of the compatible remedies. Price reduction is only provided for in sales contracts through the *quanti minoris* action (C. civ., art. 1914), and repair or replacement of defective performance is provided only in consumer rights.

Unilateral resolution is made possible in certain types of domestic contracts (insurance, supply, commercial agency, residential lease, commercial lease) and in international sales of goods adopted in 1999, always in cases of serious non-performance. However, case law and the majority doctrine currently reject the possibility of unilaterally terminating the contract as a remedy concurrent with judicial resolution.

2. PARTICULAR ASPECTS OF GOVERNMENT CONTRACTS

Administrative contracts are identified today by a subjective rather than material criterion, under the designation of "state contract," understood as including all contracts entered into by a state entity regardless of its legal regime (It should be noted that in Colombian law, the term "state" refers to the public domain, meaning it includes contracts entered into by local authorities as well). Consequently, such contracts may adopt legal regimes such as civil and commercial law governing the contractual relationship or obligatory for the contracting administration, as well as specific norms of the general law on public contracts. To this end, jurisprudence has had to establish a classification of state contracts. On the one hand, there are strictly state contracts, i.e., those whose legal regime is governed by Law 80 of 1993 on state contracts, as amended by Laws 1150 of 2007, 1474 of 2011, Decree-Law 019 of 2012, and Laws 1753 of 2015, 1882 of 2018, 1955 of 2019, 2022 of 2020, 2068, 2069, and 2080 of 2021. On the other hand, there are special state contracts, i.e., those governed by private law norms but always required to respect the general principles of administrative function, as provided in Article 209 of the 1991 Constitution: legality, morality, efficiency, economy, speed, impartiality, and publicity. Additionally, they must adhere to the principles of public resource administration set forth in Article 267 of the Constitution: efficiency, economy, fairness, and consideration of environmental costs. These special contracts must also comply with the general regime of state contracts concerning situations of lack of capacity to contract and incompatibilities for entering into contracts.

State contracts in general, but particularly those "strictly state contracts," require compliance with specific forms and formalities as mandated by law. These requirements are also demanded of special state contracts through Council of State jurisprudence, which aims to create a single category of state contracts based on the resources, objectives, and purposes involved. It should be noted that state contracts are naturally solemn, as article 41 of Law 80 of 1993 requires, for their perfection, the existence of a written document containing the description of the contractual object and the remuneration of the co-contractor.

Regarding formalities, state contracts must comply with: (1) adequate planning, as required by Decree 1082 of 2015, which involves analyzing the economic sector in which the contractual object will be acquired, determining project risks and execution, as well as clearly and precisely defining the contract's object and factors to choose the best offer according to the contracting authority's interests; (2) the fulfillment of offer selection procedures, provided in the law and manuals for authorities not subject to the general law on state contracts (these procedures culminate in the adoption of an administrative act, which awards the contract to the best offer); (3) contract subscription by signature or the conjunction of the bid and accepted offer; (4) procedures for contract legalization, including publication in the electronic system of state contracts and/or on the contracting authority's website; (5) acceptance of guarantees to cover execution risks and adoption of accounting destination certification, a precondition for starting contract execution; (6) liquidation as a final accounting operation, terminating the contractual relationship (for authorities subject to the general law on state contracts, this liquidation can be carried out unilaterally by the administration if amicable liquidation fails).

Finally, depending on their object, some "strictly state contracts" naturally allow the exercise of extensive powers to unilaterally modify, interpret, and terminate the contract, with or without fault on the part of the co-contractor. Additionally, some contracts permit the exclusive application of Colombian law and the reversion of assets at the end of the concession. Conversely, regarding "special" or broad-sense state contracts, such powers may be expressly granted to ensure unilateral continuity of the public service that is the subject of the contract or justifies public procurement.

CHAPTER TEN

DELICTUAL LIABILITY

1. LIABILITY UNDER PRIVATE LAW

Private law liability in Colombian law is governed by the texts of Book IV of the Civil Code concerning obligations in general and contracts. It requires the fulfillment of the three classic conditions of civil liability: the existence of harm as a consequence of the fault of a third party or an attributable act. Therefore, harm, fault, and causation are the three components of civil liability in Colombian law.

It is expressly cited in article 1494 of the Civil Code as one of the four sources of civil obligations: "Obligations arise either from contracts or agreements, where two or more persons agree to the same; or from a voluntary act of a person, such as the acceptance of an inheritance or legacy, or from all quasi-contracts; or as a consequence of an act which causes damage to another person, such as torts; or finally, by provision of the law, such as between parents and their children."

The texts of the Civil Code also expressly provide for a division between contractual and extra-contractual liabilities. While Title XII of Book IV of the Code regulates the effects of obligations, with all these norms making express reference to contracts, Title XXX-IV of the same book contains texts governing the issue of common law liability arising from torts and faults.

A general principle of liability for fault is established in article 2341 of the Civil Code in tort law: "Anyone who commits a tort or fault that causes harm to another is obliged to indemnify them, notwithstanding the main penalty provided by law for such tort or fault."

It should be noted that the main penalty refers to penalties of a penal nature.

This general principle is elucidated by article 63, inserted in Chapter V of the preliminary title of the Civil Code, regarding "definitions of various words frequently used," and by article 2302 concerning quasi-contracts, both providing definitions of deceit and fault. Deceit, conceived as "the positive intention to cause harm to the person or property of another" (C. civ., art. 63), would be a tort, defined as an "unlawful act committed with the intention to harm" (C. civ., art. 2302). Fault is defined in turn by article 2302 as "an act committed without the intention to harm." Article 63, however, distinguishes three categories of fault: grave, light, and very light. According to this text, a grave fault (gross negligence or *culpa lata*) occurs when "one does not give to the property of others the care that even negligent or imprudent persons normally give to their own property;" this means it consists of behavior contrary to a minimum of vigilance, for which reason the law equates it with deceit (C. civ., art. 63, para. 1).

Light fault (*negligencia leve* or *descuido ligero*) is defined in turn as "the lack of vigilance and care that people normally use in managing their own affairs." It "opposes ordinary or medium vigilance or care" (C. civ., art. 63). This text expressly provides that this category of faults should be referred to when the law uses the term "fault" without any qualifier. As for very light fault, it is defined as "the lack of a very high vigilance, which a careful person uses in managing their most important affairs. It opposes the highest care and vigilance" (C. civ., art. 63).

However, this general principle of liability based on fault has some nuances. Three groups of texts can be identified within Title XXXIV of the Civil Code. A first group, formed by articles 2341 to

2345, outlines the general principles of liability for personal acts (direct liability); a second group, composed of articles 2346, 2347, 2348, 2349, and 2352, governs the liability for acts of individuals who are under one's guardianship or who are in a subordinate relationship with one; and finally, a third group, associated with articles 2350, 2351, 2353, 2354, 2355, and 2356, governs liability for the actions of animate and inanimate things. The second and third groups of texts correspond to so-called indirect responsibilities, based on a presumption of fault (Supreme Court of Justice, civil cassation chamber, 12 May 1939; SCJ, ch. cass. civ., 18 November 1940; SCJ, ch. cass. civ., 24 June 1942; SCJ, ch. cass. civ., 3 February 1944; 18 April 1945; SCJ, ch. cass. civ., 16 December 1952). However, differences can be identified between these two regimes of indirect liability.

In the regime of liability for the acts of others, the presumption of fault may be disregarded by demonstrating the vigilant and careful behavior of the indirect respondent at the precise moment the harmful event occurred (especially regarding the liability of parents and educators for the actions of their children and students—SCJ, ch. cass. civ., 22 May 2000, exp. 6264). On the other hand, in most events of the regime of liability for the acts of things, this presumption may only be disregarded through the demonstration of a fortuitous event, a major force, a third party intervention, or the exclusive fault of the victim, which tends to align it more with a system of liability presumption (especially in the case of dangerous activities, SCJ, ch. cass. civ., 14 March 1938; SCJ, ch. cass. civ., 18 December 2012; SCJ, ch. cass. civ., 26 August 2010; liability for damages caused by violent animals—C. civ., art. 2354: SCJ, ch. cass. civ., 6 April 1989; damages caused by the collapse of a building: SCJ, general business chamber, 9 October 1963). The list of events provided in articles 2347 for liability for the acts of others and 2356 for dangerous activities is not exhaustive.

The fault or carelessness of the victim must always be considered when evaluating the damage in order to apply a reduction in compensation: "If the victim has imprudently exposed himself to damage, the assessment of the damage will be subject to a reduction" (C. civ., art. 2357). A principle of solidarity has also been instituted by the Civil Code regarding the compensation for damage: "If a tort or fault has been committed by two or more persons, each will be jointly liable for all the damage caused by the same tort or fault (...). Any fraud or deceit committed by two or more persons entitles them to the joint action provided in this article."

Regarding damage, no limitations on the nature or type of compensable harm are imposed in tort law. As for patrimonial damage, articles 1613 and 1614, which are part of Title XII related to the "effect of obligations," make express reference to it. According to article 1613: "Compensation for harm includes the loss suffered [*daño emergente*, literally 'emerging damage'] and the lost profit [*lucro cesante*, literally 'ceased profit'];" article 1614, on the other hand, defines the loss suffered as "the loss arising from the non-performance of the obligation, or from its imperfect or delayed performance," and the lost profit as "the profit or gain that ceases to be received," as a consequence of these same three situations.

Non-patrimonial or immaterial harm has experienced significant growth through case law. Recent decisions (CSJ, civ. cass. ch., 5 August 2014; CSJ, civ. cass. ch., 9 December 2013) identify three categories of immaterial harm: moral damage, defined as harm to a person's feelings and affection, manifesting in emotional suffering and pain the victim endures following the occurrence of a harmful event; societal damage, conceived as the consequences of the harm that affect the person's non-patrimonial social activity, in other words, the ability to engage in daily activities; and harm to essential legal rights of the person or to the victim's fundamental or subjective rights, specially protected by the Constitution, defined as harm to a right inherent to the human being, such as freedom, dignity, honor, reputation, image, or privacy.

Regarding the characteristics of the damage, case law traditionally requires that it be certain and direct. The loss of opportunity, traditionally compensated, is the dispossession, disappearance, or permanent deprivation of the legitimate, real, serious, and current opportunity either to obtain a profit, benefit, or advantage in the future, or to avoid a loss, dispossession, disadvantage, or even the diminishment of one's assets (CSJ, civ. cass. ch., 9 September 2010).

2. ADMINISTRATIVE LIABILITY

Since the second half of the 19th century, the recognition of Colombian State liability has been a consistent judicial principle. Initially, ordinary jurisdiction, represented by the Supreme Court, was responsible for resolving most conflicts where the State was sued under this liability. Since 1964, however, this general competence has been vested in the Council of State.

In the early rulings of the Court, liability of the National Treasury was established based on laws such as Law 60 of 1878, which held the State accountable for damages caused by armies during the civil wars of the 19th century. In this context, if the victim failed to demonstrate compliance of their claim with legal requirements, it was rejected.

During the first part of the 20th century, in the absence of specific regulations, case law applied principles of private law liability, referring to Article 19 of the 1886 Constitution, to establish State liability for damages caused to citizens. Gradually, concepts of public law were introduced to consider service fault as a general basis for State liability.

The Council of State, endowed with exceptional powers at the time, introduced the concept of "special damages" as the foundation for liability in cases where damage resulted from lawful State activities.

The 1991 Constitution incorporated into the constitutional framework the obligation of the State to compensate citizens for damages caused. Paragraph 1 of Article 90 of the Constitution establishes the elements required to admit State liability: an unlawful damage and the attribution of the damage caused by the action or omission of a public authority.

The Colombian Constitutional Court defines "unlawful damage" as one that the victim is not obliged to assume and framed within one of the liability regimes recognized by jurisprudence before 1991. The Court had developed theories of "subjective regimes" (service fault) and "objective regimes" (exceptional risk and special damage). For damage to be compensable, it must be personal and certain.

The regimes that establish State liability are as follows:

- *Service Fault*: Case law referred to service fault where "the service operated defectively, with delays, or did not function at all." Subsequently, it defined service fault as the "violation of State obligations, either through the clear violation of a norm or the violation of the State's generic function" (Council of State, Section III, 30 March 1990).

  This concept of "service fault" was enriched by constitutional mandates developed through jurisprudence, including an analysis of compliance with the obligation contained in paragraph 2 of Article 2 of the 1991 Political Constitution of Colombia, which notably led to the application of objective attribution criteria.

  Case law has ruled that "service fault" is the general regime of liability, which serves educational and preventive functions within State liability.
- *Exceptional Risk*: The notion of "exceptional risk" as a basis for liability was accepted by the Council of State in 1984, in cases where damage resulted from risky State activities.

  Recent jurisprudential developments show an increasing trend towards using this regime of liability arising from the exercise of dangerous activities, applicable to events such as damages caused by hospital infections, conflicts related to the "risk of conflict" theory (attacks on the State in the context of armed conflict), and damages caused by psychiatric patients during their hospital stays.

This demonstrates a growing trend in the use of objective liability regimes for events where damage occurs during risky activities that are not necessarily dangerous.

- *Special Damage*: This basis of liability involves abnormal and severe damage resulting from lawful State actions, causing an imbalance in public burdens. Legitimate State actions include lawful administrative acts, administrative operations, military operations, road construction, as well as damages caused by terrorist attacks.

  Compensation for victims under this liability basis is justified by principles of solidarity and equality, as damages caused to an individual by a legitimate State action disrupt the equality of all citizens in facing public burdens. Examples include damages caused by vehicle seizures, aircraft seizures by guerrillas, military installations for guerrilla attacks, the death of a volunteer transport of army troops during an ambush, damages during mandatory military service, damages caused by road construction that devalue adjacent properties, construction of bridges that depreciate or prevent commercial activity, damages caused to individuals in terrorist attacks, or the signing of international treaties.

CHAPTER ELEVEN

QUASI-CONTRACTS

The category of quasi-contracts is expressly provided for in the Colombian Civil Code as one of the sources of obligations, following the classical Justinian quadripartite division (contract, quasi-contract, tort, quasi-tort). article 1494 states that "obligations arise (...) from a voluntary act of the person who binds himself, as (...) in all quasi-contracts." Quasi-contracts are governed by Chapter XXXIII of Book IV ("General Obligations and Contracts") of the Civil Code. Article 2302, which opens this chapter, states that "obligations (...) arise, either from law or from the voluntary act of the parties" and that "if the act from which they arise is lawful, it constitutes a quasi-contract." Article 2303, in turn, lists the main types of quasi-contracts: management of affairs (*agencia oficiosa*), payment of undue, and co-ownership (*comunidad*). However, it is considered that this list is not exhaustive, since the wording of the article itself suggests that there may be others ("there are three main quasi-contracts"). Furthermore, the same Civil Code, in at least one case, recognizes another hypothesis of quasi-contract (necessary deposit for an adult who does not have free administration of his property, article 2262).

Despite its legal consecration, the usefulness and logic of the category have been subject to controversy within doctrine. It has been noted, among other things, that the notion of quasi-contract (1) would imply a misunderstanding, since it excludes, by definition, any agreement; (2) would be an erroneous notion, insofar as it brings together heterogeneous situations that have little in common; (3) would constitute an anachronistic figure, because in current practice, the fiction of its foundation would not be necessary and would lead to confusion. In fact, the majority doctrine, criticizing this category, places the legal hypotheses of quasi-contracts within other categories. For example, it is considered that the payment of undue and certain aspects of management of affairs are manifestations of the general principle of unjust enrichment, while the issue of co-ownership relates to property law and falls under a residual category, grouping together hypotheses of legal facts from which obligations arise and not sharing the characteristic element of other sources (private autonomy, damage repair, sanction for unjust enrichment without legal cause).

On its part, jurisprudence has not pronounced on the relevance of the category, limiting itself to classifying specific cases within the quasi-contract hypotheses expressly regulated by law. Moreover, it is important to note that jurisprudence has developed the principle of unjust enrichment, partly by borrowing from certain types of quasi-contracts. Unlike a significant part of doctrine, considering unjust enrichment as a source of obligations that would encompass some traditional quasi-contractual hypotheses, current jurisprudence sees unjust enrichment as a general, autonomous principle, independent of types recognized by law.

Despite the absence of a legal definition of quasi-contract, doctrine and jurisprudence agree that it involves voluntary and lawful acts by an individual which, to produce effects, do not require the will of another (legal facts or unilateral manifestations of will).

We will successively consider the fundamental aspects of the three quasi-contracts governed by the Civil Code, as well as the principle of unjust enrichment as elaborated by jurisprudence.

Management of affairs is governed by articles 2304 to 2312 of the Civil Code. It is defined as a quasi-contract "by which one who manages, without having received a mandate, the property of a person, obliges himself to that person and obliges that person in certain cases" (C. civ., art. 2304). The conditions of management of affairs are spontaneity (acting spontaneously on behalf of another), the manager's intention to manage the affairs of a third party—the managed or master of the affair, altruistic purpose (expression of an act of solidarity), and the inability of the master to manage his own affairs due to absence or material impossibility. It should be emphasized that management of affairs binds the manager and can also create obligations on the part of the master, if such management is beneficial to him.

Management of affairs is assimilated to the contract of mandate, at least regarding the obligations of the manager (C. civ., art. 2305). However, the concepts differ in that management of affairs implies the absence of consent from the master, to the extent that acts of management can have effects despite the master's explicit prohibition (C. civ., art. 2309).

The acts that constitute the object of management are not defined; however, doctrine considers these to be acts of administration as well as disposition (extinguishing a debt, selling goods likely to lose their value or disappear, or simply caring for the master's goods). For management to be constituted and to have effects, it is also necessary for the manager to be capable (relative incapacity being admitted).

As soon as the manager decides to interfere in the sphere of another, he is bound by duties. He must manage "with all the care of a prudent person" and the degree of his responsibility may vary depending on the circumstances that led him to take charge of the matter. This responsibility will be mitigated if the interests involved are exposed to an imminent danger, and limited, in this case only, to fraud and gross negligence. Conversely, it will be more intense if the manager voluntarily took charge of the management, and will even cover slight negligence, or any fault whatsoever, if he has prevented others from taking over the management (C. civ., art. 2306).

One of the most important effects of management of affairs is that the manager is obliged to continue the management he has begun and to complete it, "until the principal is able to take over himself or appoint someone else," or, in the event of the principal's death, "until the heirs take over the direction of the matter" (C. civ., art. 2307).

Finally, the manager has the duty to render an account in order to demand reimbursement from the principal for the expenses he is entitled to for his management (C. civ., art. 2312).

Similarly, obligations may arise for the principal if the requirement of the usefulness of the management is met, when the matter has been well administered. This results in two effects: the principal must reimburse the manager for all useful or necessary expenses, and remains bound by the commitments the manager has made on his behalf towards third parties (C. civ., art. 2308, para. 1). In all cases, the management is free of charge (C. civ., art. 2308, para. 2). Effects are also recognized against the principal if the management was carried out against his will: when it has indeed been useful, the judge may grant a delay for the payment to the manager, based on considerations of equity in view of the circumstances of the principal's situation (C. civ., art. 2309).

Article 2322 of the Civil Code states that "the joint ownership (*comunidad*) of a universal or singular thing between two or more persons, without any of them having constituted a company, or celebrated another agreement related to the same thing, is a type of quasi-contract." This notion is referred by doctrine and jurisprudence to the field of property law, particularly as a modality of ownership, which is why only some fundamental aspects will be noted here.

Joint ownership is considered a quasi-contract since, even though it is akin to a company, it presupposes the absence of an agreement or contract between the co-owners. Thus, obligations arise between them because they find themselves involuntarily co-owners of a thing. Moreover, joint ownership can concern a universal thing (joint ownership of heirs over the inheritance) or a singular thing (e.g., adjudication of a building to several people).

The legal situation of the co-owners regarding the common property is governed by the principle that each must contribute to the works and repairs, as well as the one asserting that they are entitled to the fruits, in proportion to their share (C. civ., arts. 2327 and 2328). Furthermore, the obligations that each co-owner assumes within the framework of the joint ownership only bind the one who assumed them; he, in turn, will have a reimbursement action against the joint ownership. It should also be noted that in the obligations due between co-owners, the share of the insolvent co-owner will burden the shares of the others (C. civ., art. 2329). In any case, none of the co-owners is obliged to remain in the joint ownership: he can request the material division or the sale of his share, so that the proceeds are distributed (C. civ., art. 2334).

Governed by articles 2313 to 2321 of the Civil Code, the payment of the undue is considered a manifestation of the principle of unjust enrichment. Article 2313 states that "if the one who pays by mistake proves that the payment was not due, he may demand its restitution." Doctrine and jurisprudence have derived three constitutive elements from this: an effective payment made by the solvens, made by mistake, and the absence of a legal basis (absence of debt).

Regarding the requirement of error, the principle is that any payment presupposes a pre-existing obligation that serves as its cause; failing this, the payment cannot be valid (noting that payment made in view of a natural obligation is considered valid, as in this case, it cannot be reclaimed (C. civ., art. 2314)). The error can be factual or legal (C. civ., art. 2315). The burden of proof of the error lies with the solvens: if the *accipiens* attests to the existence of the payment, it must be proven to be undue, but if the *accipiens* denies the payment, its existence must be proven, only then will it be presumed undue (C. civ., art. 2316). In all cases, it should be noted that if, after erroneous payment of the debt by the *solvens*, the *accipiens* destroys the title allowing him to recover his credit, the latter will not be obliged to return what was received, the *solvens* being able to initiate the actions that the creditor had against the debtor (C. civ., art. 2313, para. 2).

On the absence of a legal basis, doctrine and jurisprudence have identified two categories: (1) the obligation serving as cause is totally non-existent or disappears subsequently (objective nature of the undue payment); (2) the error concerns the person, either the payment is made (by the debtor or a third party) to the benefit of someone who is not the creditor, or the payer mistakenly believes he is the debtor and pays someone else's debt (subjective nature of the undue payment).

Several effects result from the undue payment, the main one being the obligation of restitution from the accipiens to the solvens. But its scope depends on the good or bad faith of the *accipiens*: if he is in good faith, he is not required to return the fruits (C. civ., art. 2318), nor is he responsible for deteriorations or losses, unless they have enriched him (C. civ., art. 2319); if he has sold the thing, he only needs to return the sale price (C. civ., art. 2320); whereas if he is in bad faith, he must return the fruits, is held responsible for losses, and, if he has sold the thing, must repair the total value of the property and the damages caused.

Even if unjust enrichment is not expressly enshrined in the Civil Code (while it has been integrated into the Commercial Code of 1971, art. 831), this principle has been developed by jurisprudence since the first half of the 19th century. Although it is not a quasi-contract in the proper sense, the fact that jurisprudence has recognized it from certain concepts governed by law and considered as applications of this principle, such as quasi-contracts like the undue payment or management of affairs, justifies a brief mention in this study.

Jurisprudence has stated that "unjust enrichment lies in the general principle of law that no one may enrich themselves at the expense of another" and requires, for the corresponding action to succeed, the following elements: enrichment (obtaining a patrimonial advantage, negative or positive), a correlative impoverishment (transfer of value from one patrimony to another, originating from the same event), and the absence of a just cause. Moreover, from a procedural point of view, unjust enrichment can only exist when there is no "other action deriving from a contract, quasi-contract, tort, or quasi-tort, or those arising from absolute rights." The action is therefore subsidiary in nature, and to this extent, unjust enrichment is considered an autonomous source of obligations.

CHAPTER TWELVE

BUSINESS ENTITIES

1. FORMS OF BUSINESS ENTITIES

1.1 SOLE TRADER

Commercial activity can be carried out by natural persons, either directly or through an intermediary, either in their own name or on behalf of third parties, and risks can be covered by dedicated assets or by sole proprietorships with limited liability.

1.2 TRADING AS A COMPANY/CORPORATION

In Colombia, corporate law regulates companies, meaning that only types of companies explicitly provided for by the legislature exist. The Commercial Code provides for five types of companies: general partnership; limited partnership, either simple or with shares; limited liability company; and corporation. Additionally, in 2008, an additional form was created: the simplified corporation.

The corporate forms provided for in the Commercial Code originate from a contract; thus, article 98 of the Code lists as essential elements of the corporate legal act: plurality of persons, financial contributions, and distribution of profits from the activity it will develop.

The common feature of all types of companies, as provided for in the Commercial Code, once the company is established, is the creation of a legal entity independent of the individual partners. The formal requirements of the Code demand, both for their formation and subsequent amendment, the drafting of a public deed executed before a notary and registered with the commercial registry maintained by the chambers of commerce.

Therefore, corporate acts that meet the essential elements but do not comply with formal or publicity requirements will either produce a *de facto* company lacking legal personality or a company not enforceable against third parties.

The main characteristics of each type of company under Colombian law are as follows:

The general partnership is characterized by being a closed and personal partnership. For its establishment, a minimum of two partners is required, who in exchange for their contributions will receive a share of interest. These interests cannot be cumulative, so each partner will have only one, with its value being higher or lower depending on each partner's economic contribution. Their availability is limited, so that upon sale, the statutes must be reformed.

The liability regime applicable to partners of general partnerships entails joint and several liability towards third parties if the company's assets are insufficient to pay its debts. In this type of company, all partners are legally entitled to represent the company, and decisions are made at a partners' meeting (board of directors) by a majority of its members. Statute reforms and the delegation of management to a third party require unanimous approval, underscoring its personal nature.

The limited liability company, on the other hand, requires a minimum of two partners and a maximum of 25 for its establishment. The share capital is divided into equal social quotas and can be cumulative to represent each partner's contribution. Disposal actions of social quotas also lead to statutory reforms, which only require the affirmative vote of a plural number of partners holding at least 70% of the quotas into which the social capital is divided. Although the liability regime of partners is limited to the amount of their contributions, they may, through rules outside the corporate law framework, be jointly liable for obligations arising from relationships with workers or tax debts.

The limited partnership can take two different forms. On the one hand, there are the general partners who gave rise to the company's formation, are responsible for managing it, and have a liability regime like that of general partnership partners. On the other hand, there are the limited partners, who are investors and do not have the mandate to manage the company, so their liability is limited to the amount of their contributions. Regarding simple limited partnerships, the contributions of limited partners are represented in social quotas; for limited partnerships with shares, partners receive shares. Reforms to the statutes in these types of companies require approval from both types of partners, but also require a special majority for limited partners.

Additionally, the corporation is provided for by the Commercial Code. This form of company requires a minimum of five shareholders for its establishment. The structure of a corporation is more complex: in addition to a shareholders' assembly, it includes an intermediate management body called the board of directors, a legal representative, and a supervisory body (equivalent to a supervisory board, called an "auditor").

The liability regime of shareholders in a corporation is strictly limited to the contributions represented by shares. All shares have the same value, can be cumulative, and their sale does not lead to a statutory reform, as it suffices to apply rules for the circulation of securities with corporate content. The valid quorum generally requires a plurality of shareholders, representing the majority of the shares composing the company's capital, and decisions are made by the majority of shareholders present.

Moreover, the simplified joint-stock company, created in 2008, is a more flexible form under the Commercial Code rules, especially concerning its establishment and operation. To this end, the simplified joint-stock company can be established by a unilateral legal act, with no requirement for a public written deed. Depending on the nature of the assets contributed, registering the deed with the commercial registry will also grant legal personality.

The share capital of a simplified joint-stock company is represented by equal-value shares, similar to corporations, but its organizational structure is much less complex. Indeed, the simplified joint-stock company is not required to have either a board of directors or a supervisory board, unless otherwise stated or in accounting provisions. In general, and unlike what is provided for in the Commercial Code, Law 1258 of 2008 establishes a non-exhaustive and supplementary regime for this type of company, allowing greater flexibility in its bylaws. Furthermore, among all the changes brought about by this law, it should be noted the elimination of *ultra vires* doctrine (legal acts that engage the company in commercial or economic activities beyond its corporate purpose) and the possibility of an indefinite duration of the "social contract."

Lastly, there are some particular regulations applicable to companies when their capital contains contributions made by the State or according to the activity they carry out, or if they form an organized group of companies. In these cases, the legislation provides special rules for mixed economy companies, companies providing public services, and groups of companies.

2. DIFFICULTIES ENCOUNTERED BY BUSINESS ENTERPRISES

The Colombian insolvency regime is divided into two parts. The first, contained in Law 1116 of 2006, applies to companies, natural persons engaged in commercial activities, and generally to legal entities conducting economic activities. The second part refers to the insolvency of non-trading natural persons, regulated by the General Procedure Code (*Codigo General del Proceso*), contained in Law 1564 of 2012.

There are two types of mechanisms: one aimed at restructuring and safeguarding the company or, in general, the debtor's economic activity, through the conclusion of an agreement defining new conditions to ensure compliance with obligations. The second is a liquidation mechanism, which aims to extinguish the debtor's obligations through the sale or auction of assets to creditors, up to the value of these assets, in accordance with the rules of legal preference.

These regimes generally aim to protect credit, safeguard and restructure the enterprise as a source of wealth, as well as preserve employment, objectives recognized by Colombian jurisprudence that guide the application of various rules.

The authorities responsible for managing insolvencies include, on one hand, the Superintendence of Companies (*Superintendencia de Sociedades*), an administrative entity attached to the national government, which, under a legal mandate and in accordance with constitutional provisions, assumes jurisdictional functions and can be petitioned by companies, branches of foreign companies, and natural persons, at their discretion. On the other hand, the Civil Circuit Judges (*Jueces Civiles de Circuito*) handle insolvency cases of legal entities other than companies, as well as natural persons, at their discretion.

Furthermore, the insolvency of natural persons falls under accredited and authorized conciliation centers, as well as notaries, within the framework of restructuring mechanisms. Liquidation is the responsibility of municipal civil judges.

From article 47 onwards, Law 1116 of 2006 establishes the final formula for the insolvency regime of companies: the so-called "judicial liquidation" procedure, which aims to swiftly and orderly liquidate the debtor's assets, maximizing the proceeds from the sale of its assets and favoring the overall sale of the organization.

Its scope includes natural persons engaged in commercial activities, legal entities without a special liquidation regime, branches of foreign companies, and autonomous assets intended for economic activities. The competent entities vary; for for-profit legal entities and branches of foreign companies, there is a specialized entity that exceptionally assumes jurisdictional functions: the Superintendence of Companies. Furthermore, liquidations concerning non-profit legal entities and autonomous assets intended for economic activities fall under the jurisdiction of Civil Circuit

Judges. A natural person engaged in commercial activities has the right, according to the legislator, to petition either the Superintendence of Companies or the Civil Circuit Judge at the debtor's place of residence.

The legislator has designed a system as objective as possible, which triggers direct access to the liquidation solution without exhausting the prior negotiation avenues provided for in Law 1116. Scenarios such as abandoning business management, failure to comply with certain procedural obligations during restructuring negotiations, and non-payment of privileged debts immediately trigger the opening of the liquidation procedure.

The formal documents to be annexed include the annual accounts and explanations of the reasons leading to insolvency, in anticipation of a declaration of disqualification from conducting commercial activities. Legitimate petitioners include, besides official surveillance entities, in expressly defined cases, the debtor and creditors holding unpaid claims, as well as the representative of an insolvency procedure abroad, according to cross-border insolvency rules.

Once the facts and formal documents are examined, the judge in charge of the collective procedure issues an order, not subject to appeal, to open the judicial liquidation procedure, a decision that defines the boundary between claims included in the collective procedure and other claims, in accordance with Law 1116 of 2006. At this stage, personal, patrimonial, and contractual formalities of the safeguard procedure are put in place, materialized in instruments and specific measures pronounced by the judge in the opening decision of the procedure.

Regarding the procedure structure itself, the order opening the procedure, materializing the initial effects of judicial liquidation, must be registered in the commercial registry and notified by notice within twenty days. From that moment, creditors have a fixed period to present at least summary evidence of their claims; similarly, the liquidator initiates operations within their purview, namely preparing the qualification of claims and determining voting rights, as well as conducting an inventory of the debtor's assets for expert evaluation.

Once these operations are completed, the draft judgment is communicated, allowing all creditors and interested parties to raise objections.

At this stage of the procedure, three alternatives are possible: either creditors and interested parties have no objections, objections are raised but reconciliation is sufficient to overcome them, or these objections persist despite attempts at reconciliation.

In any case, it is during a hearing that the qualification of claims, determination of votes, and properly evaluated inventory begin. The direct sale stage of the debtor's assets commences, lasting a maximum of two months, after which the adjudication agreement is prepared, with interesting specifics. Thus, the rule of preference rights requires the liquidator to first make payments in cash, then auction real estate, followed by movable property, and finally pay those with intangible assets, creditors holding lower ranks in the preferential list.

The legislator has provided a series of rules designed to prevent delays caused by notarial registration procedures, tax issues, and reluctance to hand over and/or physically receive adjudicated goods from unjustifiably prolonging the procedure.

Finally, the law dedicates the last stage of the procedure to studying a detailed report of operations conducted by the liquidator and the rendering of accounts, which are communicated and subject to challenge. Ultimately, with the judge's approval, the liquidation procedure concludes, noting that it may also lead to the conclusion of a reorganization agreement and the possibility of additional adjudications once the judicial liquidation procedure is completed.

During the economic crisis triggered by the Covid-19 pandemic, the Colombian government issued two decrees to streamline procedures. On one hand, Decree 560 of 2020 establishes two new business reorganization procedures: "emergency negotiation," expected to last three months, and "business resumption," before chambers of commerce. However, the new regulations also include additional tools to support the sustainability of viable enterprises. On the other hand, Decree 772 of 2020 established two processes for micro and small enterprises: "abbreviated reorganization" and "simplified liquidation," aiming to limit procedural delays. Thus, under the new regulations, processes are simpler and faster, with emergency negotiations expected to conclude within a maximum of three months.

3. FRAMEWORK OF BUSINESS ACTIVITIES

While Colombia governed this area since 1982 through a Consumer Statute, which outlined the principles, rules, and procedures aimed at giving effect to consumer rights, the Political Constitution, starting in 1991, included in the title of rights a provision explicitly referring to the quality of goods and services, the information that must be provided to consumers, the liability of producers and sellers, as well as the right of everyone to participate in consumer associations.

In line with the provisions of the constitutional order and the progress in consumer sector relations, Law 1480 of 2011 was enacted. This law created the current Consumer Statute (*Estatuto del Consumidor*), which has become the fundamental norm of consumer law.

The said Statute contains substantive and procedural rules in this regard.

Regarding substantive rules, it regulates: general principles concerning consumer rights; consumer rights and duties; quality, conformity, safety, and warranties; information and advertising; contractual protection of consumers including general conditions, adhesion contracts, abusive clauses; transactions carried out with financing systems; distance sales or those using non-traditional means; consumer protection in electronic commerce; and a national quality subsystem.

Regarding the substantive rules of this regime, the following characteristics are noteworthy:

- Except in the presence of competent authorities specifically responsible for consumer protection, the competent authority is the Superintendence of Industry and Commerce. The law also provides for specific exceptions, where competence has been assigned to other authorities; for example, in the field of public utility services or financial services, other superintendencies supervise each sector (the Superintendence of Public Services and the Superintendence of Finance).
- Consumers have two different avenues to exercise their rights, depending on the legal interest sought for protection. If it is a general problem, an administrative procedure is initiated with the corresponding executive branch authority; if the legal interest is specific, such as claiming a warranty right, the process is judicial, and therefore, it is the judges of the Republic or, as applicable, the Superintendence of Industry and Commerce who handle it.
- Consumer law applies to both public and private law institutions. "Indeed, the liability scheme regarding adequacy, quality, and safety of goods and services includes liability towards the consumer; damages caused by a defective product fall under private law; as well as aspects requiring state intervention regarding the safety of products offered to consumers, through technical regulations and administrative procedures initiated to ensure compliance, falling under administrative oversight..." (C. Caycedo, "Principios e instituciones del Derecho de Protección del Consumidor en Colombia. Lineamientos del Sistema Legal de protección a consumidores y usuarios en Colombia, conforme con la doctrina Constitucional y de Casación Civil," in *Ligia Valderrama Rojas C.* (dir.), *Perspectivas del Derecho del consumo*, ed. Universidad Externado de Colombia, 2013).

CHAPTER THIRTEEN

LABOR AND EMPLOYMENT LAW

In Colombia, as in most countries in the Americas, labor standards are enshrined in the Constitution. Article 53 of the Constitution sets forth the fundamental principles governing labor relations. The most important of these are: "equality of rights for workers; minimum, vital, and progressive remuneration, proportionate to the quantity and quality of work; job security; the non-availability of legal minimums for social benefits; recourse to settlement or conciliation in case of disputes over certain rights; the principle of favorability for the interpretation and application of the most favorable norm; the primacy of reality imposed on the formalities provided for subjects of labor relations; the right to social security, training, and necessary rest; special protection for women, maternity, and underage workers."

Furthermore, this same Article 53 provides that the State must ensure timely payment, as well as periodic adjustment of pensions. It should also be noted that international labor conventions ratified by Colombia are an integral part of national legislation.

The fact that these fundamental labor principles have constitutional status has three consequences: (1) they prevail over other legal norms and thereby determine the relevance and validity of other norms, rules, or decisions of authorities; (2) they are legal sources of direct and immediate application in domestic law; (3) the interpretation drawn from them takes precedence over other labor law norms (Constitutional Court, Judgment T-406/1992).

Constitutional jurisprudence has given broad scope to these principles, leading to their application in all forms of labor relations, in accordance with Article 25 of the Constitution, which states that "labor is a right and an obligation, and in all its modalities, it is subject to state protection." This has resulted in an impressive volume of tutela judgments (a category of judgments by the Constitutional Court concerning the protection of fundamental rights), in which the Court relies on constitutional labor principles, such as maternity protection, vital minimum, and stability, as a basis for disputes concerning independent workers or associated labor cooperatives.

Regarding the direct applicability of ratified international labor treaties by Colombia, they are an integral part of national legislation. Similarly, certain international conventions may be incorporated into the constitutional block, established by the Colombian Constitutional Court in 1995 (Judgment C-225/1995). This is particularly the case for treaties aimed at protecting human rights. They suffer no restrictions, including in cases of states of emergency, provided they are ratified (Constitution, Art. 93).

The incorporation of labor into the constitutional block has allowed for the jurisprudential development of rights and guarantees for Colombian workers. Many legal provisions contrary to international treaties have been declared unconstitutional (especially in the field of collective labor law, some norms of which were established in the mid-20th century by an interventionist state towards union movements), while others have been declared constitutional but conditional, insofar as they adhere to the interpretation of the Constitutional Court, without affecting constitutional rights, principles, and values (job security, progressive economic, social, and cultural rights, as well as equality in labor).

Finally, several *tutela* judgments concerning social security rights have taken into account the principles of Article 53 of the Colombian Constitution, as well as the norms of the constitutional block. In these decisions, the Court has pronounced immediate and direct application, regardless of the status of benefits present in the case (vital minimum, non-availability, equality, etc.).

1. INDIVIDUAL RELATIONSHIPS

The employment contract is a bilateral agreement between an employer (legal or natural person) and an employee (who must be a natural person), with the purpose of providing personal and subordinate services, in exchange for a salary (*Código Sustantivo del Trabajo*—CST, art. 22).

For its formation, the law requires three elements: the personal provision of the service, legal subordination, and payment of a salary (CST, art. 23). Any personal provision of service leads to a simple presumption of subordination, allowing for the demonstration of the existence of an employment relationship (CST, art. 24).

Regarding the classification of employment contracts, the CST recognizes four types: indefinite-term contract or CDI (CST, arts. 37, *et seq.*); fixed-term contract or CDD (CST, art. 46); contract for the duration of a specific work previously determined or CDO (CST, arts. 37, *et seq.*); temporary, occasional, or accidental contract, called CTOA (CST, art. 6).

The CDI requires no specific formalities; it is indeed a consensual contract. The parties need only determine and agree on the conditions of work. The CDD, on the other hand, is a formal contract; its validity depends both on its written form and on compliance with a maximum duration limit (which is set by law at three years). There are two types of CDD based on their duration: the first cannot exceed one year, while the second can last up to three years. The third contract mentioned is the CDO, which does not depend on any formality. This contract is entered into for the execution of specific work or a specific task and ends only upon completion of that task. The last of these contracts, the CTOA, has a maximum duration of one month and its purpose is to perform work different from the usual tasks assigned by the employer.

In Colombian law, beyond the traditional obligations already mentioned, the CST details other specific obligations. This includes, for example, good faith obligations for both parties (CST, art. 55), loyalty and obedience for the employee, as well as security and protection for the employer (CST, art. 56). Other obligations, which in comparative law would fall under internal regulations, are also mentioned in the CST, such as the obligation to take care of work tools or refrain from consuming alcohol at the workplace (CST, arts. 57, 58, 59, and 60).

Another category of obligations is related to the social protection of the employee. In this regard, the employer must finance a number of legally determined social benefits. These can be improved through collective rights associated with work (such as the right to company social protection). Examples of these benefits include: transportation assistance (Law 15 of 1959); unemployment assistance, known as *cesantías* (CST, art. 249); interest on these assistance payments (Law 52 of 1975 and Law 50 of 1990, art. 99); service bonus (CST, art. 306); provision of clothing and shoes (CST, art. 230); old-age pensions, health benefits, and occupational hazards; payment of parafiscal obligations.

Regarding working hours, these are legally fixed at forty-eight hours per week. Colombian employees also have a right to vacation, with the law providing for fifteen days of annual leave (CST, art. 161). The law also regulates overtime, night work, Sunday work, and holidays (CST, arts. 168, *et seq.*).

Concerning the termination of the employment contract, the will of the parties prevails, unless the termination of the employment relationship is due to objective circumstances such as force majeure or the definitive and involuntary closure of the business (CST, art. 61). When termination results from the employer's initiative, except in cases of maternity, disability, or union protection, the employer may terminate the contract without just cause and without judicial or administrative authorization, in exchange for compensation as provided for in the CST, which depends on the type of employment contract (CST, art. 64).

For their part, the employee can resign without notice. However, their departure must not cause damage to the company. However, if it is demonstrated that their departure is linked to legal or contractual violations by the employer, this termination will be reclassified as dismissal without just cause (CST, art. 62).

After the termination of the contract, certain obligations persist. Non-payment of wages and social benefits results in the judicial imposition of a special indemnity, called *moratoria* (CST, art. 65). Similarly, non-payment of certain benefits leads to special sanctions (Law 50 of 1990, for example, art. 99).

2. COLLECTIVE BARGAINING

The norms governing union representation and the framework for collective bargaining are contained in the Constitution, the CST, and various regulatory decrees.

At first glance, the Colombian legal system appears to favor union representation for conducting negotiations. Furthermore, it privileges enterprise-level union negotiations over other negotiation levels. However, the amendments made to the CST in the last fifteen years, under the influence of decisions from the Constitutional Court, indicate that the framework for collective bargaining in Colombia has become fragmented and atomized. This situation has immediately resulted in a proliferation of micro-unions, to the detriment of larger organizations. As a consequence, the rule of majority representation is nearly overshadowed. It is not an exaggeration to consider that while the effect of judgments regarding union rights is undeniable, it has unfortunately been devastating for collective bargaining in Colombian enterprises.

Yet, articles 357-1, 357-2, 357-3, 360, and 376 of the CST uphold principles of collective labor law, such as the prohibition of pluralism within the same enterprise, the majority representation rule, the principle of union unity, and the prohibition of employee syndical transhumance among unions in the same sector. However, these articles now have no effect due to decisions of unconstitutionality rendered by the Constitutional Court (decisions C-567 of 2000 dated 17 May 2000; C-797 of 2000 dated 19 June 2000; and C-063 of 2008 dated 30 January 2008). Consequently, without any normative foundation, an infinite number of unions can coexist within the same enterprise, with employees changing their union affiliation as they see fit. All these unions can participate in negotiations and sign any conceivable type of agreement. Moreover, each union can negotiate independently, where a unified negotiation with all unions would have been necessary.

Decree 89 of 2014 attempted, unsuccessfully, to unify union negotiations. It proposed that union organizations voluntarily adopt a single list of demands and engage in collective bargaining involving all unions simultaneously.

However, it must be acknowledged that this cacophony is less pronounced in the public sector. Negotiations there involve all unions, thus avoiding separate negotiations as permitted under applicable provisions for employees and civil servants.

In conclusion, the interpretation by the constitutional court in the aforementioned judgments, far from constituting a social advancement capable of strengthening union unity and developing union negotiation, corresponds more to a setback that undermines union powers and hinders their action in society. Therefore, it is more necessary than ever for the legislature to take the initiative for comprehensive reform in the framework of collective negotiations in Colombia, taking into account the general and predominant criteria of the ILO.